The Official

Family Guide to Tee Ball

Bing Broido

A Division of Howard W. Sams & Company
A Bell Atlantic Company

Published by Masters Press (A Division of Howard W. Sams &
Co., A Bell Atlantic Company)
2647 Waterfront Pkwy. E. Dr., Suite 300
Indianapolis, IN 46214

Published 1996

Printed in the United States of America

96 97 98 99 00 01 02   10 9 8 7 6 5 4 3 2 1

Library of Congress Cataloging-in-Publication

Broido, Bing
    The official T-ball USA family guide to tee ball / Bing Broido.
        p. cm.
    ISBN: 1-57028-082-7 (alk. paper)
    1. T-ball. 2. T-ball--Psychological aspects. I. T-Ball USA
(Organization) II. Title.

GV881.5.B76 1996
796.357'8--dc20   96-24698
                                                          CIP

The T•BALL USA ASSOCIATION is the national not-for-profit youth sports organization dedicated to the development of the game of T-Ball. Its objectives are to:

- ■ Furnish benefits to national youth baseball leagues, local organizers, parents and youngsters that enhance the quality of the game and the playing experience.

- ■ Stimulate participation by young boys and girls in an early-age organized team game and instill a foundation for sportsmanship, fair play and teamwork.

- ■ Bring together community and parent groups, municipal departments or agencies, service organizations and leagues now involved or interested in the sport so that the game may be played in an informed and consistent manner in all parts of the country.

- ■ Provide communications and guidelines for those responsible for the local administration of the game and for the families they serve.

- ■ Recommend rules of play and playing procedures.

- ■ Establish equipment specifications.

- ■ Create an avenue of support by companies interested in advancing youth and family-oriented activities.

- ■ Publicize and promote the sport and its sponsors in all appropriate media.

The T•BALL USA™ logo will be used to identify the projects and services created to foster national and local programs, mark the official licensed products and corporate sponsorships and serve as a badge of belonging for the participants and their families.

T•BALL USA ASSOCIATION, INC.
Suite 1901
915 Broadway
New York, NY 10010
Tel: 800/741-0845 • FAX: 212/254-8042
Bing Broido, President • Lois Richards, Vice President

Acknowledgments

I want to thank each of the contributors of articles in the Information and Advice section; the T-Ball league administrators, staff, municipal recreation/youth sports directors and parents who responded to our activity survey and other questions; and the following individuals who helped make this book a reality:

Chuck Alley	Abraham Key
Richard W. Case	Bruno Dov Lerer
Wayne Christensen	Garry McNabb
James R. Corbett	Marion P. Pearson
John Doleva	Helen M. Piessens
Marthe Dubroy	Jim Rooney
Fred Engh	Nick Senter
Douglas J. Gaynor	Wes Skelton
Dan Gliniecki	Al Stein
Larry Green	Dennis Sullivan
Dayton Hobbs	Brad Sweeney
Paul W. Homer	Ronald Tellefsen
Dick Jones	Ken Tetreault

Special thanks to the kids in the photos, whose faces reflect the fun and excitement of playing T-Ball; my family and friends for their patience and support; and the team at Masters Press, especially Tom Bast, Holly Kondras and Kim Heusel.

Dedication

To Alana and Jack and their generation.

T•BALL USA photo

Credits

Photography, except where otherwise credited, by Gene Sowell.
Field of play illustration by Elmer Wexler.
Text layout by Kim Heusel
Cover design by Phil Velikan
Edited by Kim Heusel

Photo courtesy BIKE Athletic Company

Table of Contents

Introduction

In my years with the Dodger organization, I have had opportunities to watch youngsters learn about the game, teamwork and life. T-Ball is a fabulous way to introduce the game and to develop the personal skills and attitudes that can mean success in sports and life.

—Tommy Lasorda, manager

T-Ball is the entry sport to baseball and softball for youngsters, primarily, five through eight years old and has become a major youth recreational activity. The elimination of pitching and any fear of being hit by a pitched ball allows organized team participation at an early age. Young players learn the fundamentals and develop baseball skills in minimally competitive league play. The emphasis is on hitting, running, fielding and throwing in an action game that combines fun and teamwork.

History: Branch Rickey, the owner of the Brooklyn Dodgers in the early 1950s, is credited with the introduction of a flexible batting tee made from an automobile radiator hose. It was used for practice by the great stars of that era, such as Jackie Robinson, Duke Snider and Gil Hodges. Rules for a tee-based game followed and, using a tee adapted from an inflation cup, a cow milking device, the sport was widely played in Canada during the 1960s. Little League Baseball has offered T-Ball as an early learning experience for basic baseball skills and the game provides a natural transition to its minor-league program. Other national and regional youth baseball organizations include T-Ball in their programs: the Bambino Division of Babe Ruth, the Shetland and Pinto leagues of PONY

Baseball, the Farm League in Dizzy Dean Baseball, the "A" Division of Dixie Youth Baseball, etc.

YMCA Sports and municipal park and recreation departments in communities of all sizes were early organizers and/or providers for local league play and continue to be a most important part of the game. A wide variety of independent parent groups have created and fostered the growth of T-Ball in their localities and bring a special vitality and passion to the game.

T-Ball is played in every state and many foreign countries. The U.S. constituency includes league organizers, administrators and staff, volunteers, officials, managers, coaches, local sponsors and the friends, parents and players from the nearly 16 million families with boys and girls of T-Ball age. As the game is the first organized sport for most children, there is a very high level of parent involvement and participation.

Local groups often develop their own playing rules; until now, there has been no standardization of the regulations and equipment so that the game can be played in an identical manner throughout the country by all types of youth-oriented organizations. The major differences in play concern winning/losing and what constitutes an inning. Many leagues do keep score and have one team win. Other leagues position the game as a learning experience that is fun, builds skills, develops a sense of teamwork with excitement for all, and do not determine a winner or loser. Some leagues consider an inning to be the traditional three outs; most prefer to have each team "bat around" where an inning ends when every player has batted one time. Coach-pitch (where an adult throws the ball to the batter) is becoming more popular for the older players whose hitting skills have been developed.

The more structured national and regional organizations are beginning to state that their long-established rules are not mandatory but open to local option allowing communities to determine the best regulations for their games. T•BALL USA has developed suggested rules of play (beginning on page 107) based on the advice of many organizers, coaches and parents.

Babe Ruth said, "Start them when they're young. Teach them to play when they're four years old." Organized T-Ball has responded in a meaningful manner, providing an avenue for boys and girls to begin their baseball experience and establishing a pattern of participation and pleasure for the years that follow.

This book is a guide not only for families already involved but also interested in becoming a part of T-Ball activity. Local league organizers, staff and coaches (often parents) will also benefit from the experiences and advice from other communities. The game, however played, is intended as a way for children to have fun, develop basic skills and a sense of teamwork. T-Ball is a game for the entire family to enjoy.

Information
and
Advice

Letter to Parents

Dick Jones, Associate Director of Sports, YMCA of the USA

The YMCA of the USA is pleased to announce it has established a collaborative relationship with T•BALL USA. Through this relationship, T•BALL USA is providing YMCAs with materials, products and equipment to help it enhance its T-Ball programs.

The goals of YMCA youth sports are to:

■ Build self-esteem.

■ Teach values, communication and human relations skills.

■ Teach physical skills, fitness and health.

■ Develop responsibility and decision making skills.

■ Enhance leadership skills in youth and adults.

■ Build relationships among peers, and between parent and child.

■ Support and strengthen family life.

■ Create a fun experience for children and their families.

These goals are based upon certain beliefs about youth sports, a philosophy summarized in these eight concepts:

Participation. Everyone plays!

Fun. We play sports to have fun!

Fitness. Regular cardiovascular exercise is important for a lifetime!

Skills. Emphasize the fundamentals!

Teamwork. Focus on cooperation, not competition!

Fair play. Fair play involves respect!

Family involvement. Youth sports is a family program!

Volunteers. Volunteers are the key!

T•BALL USA is to be commended for its efforts to standardize the rules of play and playing procedures, establish equipment specifications, instill a foundation for sportsmanship, fair play and teamwork in young boys and girls; and publicize and promote the sport and its sponsors in all appropriate media.

Please check with your local YMCA to see if T-Ball is available in your community.

Mr. Jones is the Associate Director of Sports for the YMCA of the USA. His responsibilities include developing resources and coordinating training for youth sport programs, serving as liaison to the United States Olympic Committee and national governing bodies for sport in the country, and overall administration and management of national YMCA sports programs.

Kids & T-Ball:
What's a Parent to Do?

Darrell J. Burnett, Ph.D.

"If a kid can't have fun playin' ball, then what's the point of playin'?"
> — *75-year-old great-grandfather of a T-ball player, concerned that organized sports are taking the joy and spontaneity out of youth sports*

T-Ball: The Entry Sport

T-Ball is the entry sport to baseball and softball. Notice the word *entry*. It's significant. A young kid's initial experience with a sport can determine whether that kid will continue to play that sport in future years. Recent surveys back up the wisdom in the quote of the great-grandpa noted above. They show that the No. 1 reason kids play sports at a recreational level is to have fun! It's the fun that keeps them coming back.

Surveys have also shown that one of the main reasons kids continue to play sports is positive parent interaction! So, one of our main goals as parents of T-Ballers is do everything we can to make it a fun experience for them and to try to stay positive in our interactions with them as they experience the wonderful world of T-Ball.

T-Ball: A Self-Esteem Enhancer

T-Ball is a great opportunity for us, as parents, to help our kids develop a strong sense of self-esteem. Think about it. Research tells us that there are four cornerstones to the development of self-esteem: A sense of BELONGING; a sense of feeling WORTHWHILE just as a person, regardless of looks, talent or wealth; a sense of

5

DIGNITY, being treated with respect, without humiliation or sarcasm; and a sense of being in CONTROL of one's environment, future and destiny.

Belonging   Worthiness

(What kids **hear** about themselves
is the basis for their self-view.)

Self-Esteem

(Kids usually **screen out** whatever
doesn't match their self-image.)

Dignity   Control

The Four Cornerstones of Self-Esteem

T-Ball contributes to each of these cornerstones. There's nothing quite like having a team uniform, a team name and a team identity to give a kid a strong sense of **belonging**. In my early days of T-Ball coaching, I had one kid sleep in his uniform the first day he got it. I had another say, "I'm on a team, I've got a uniform, now I'm a real person!"

As for feeling **worthwhile** just as a person, T-Ball guarantees that everybody plays, regardless of skills. Every player is guaranteed to bat and play. A sense of **dignity** is also maintained through T-Ball because the emphasis is on positive coaching, with no public humiliation of players through remarks or taunting.

And finally, a sense of **control** begins to develop through T-Ball as the youngsters develop confidence and control by learning how to use the equipment (bats, balls, gloves), by learning the basic rules and by learning how to be in control of their emotions, from tears to temper tantrums, as they interact with other players, take turns and play as a team.

The few months of T-Ball life can be a great opportunity for building some positive memories for our kids and for our family life. To stay focused on our task as parents, here are a few reminders. Think of the word T B-A-L-L P-A-R-E-N-T

Think *positives*

It is said that, in the early, formative years, children's self views are based upon what they hear about themselves from the adults in their lives, especially their parents. It makes sense, then, that we, as parents, make every effort to think of ways to communicate positives to our kids, and to make sure they hear those positives — on the field or off. The idea is to catch our kids doing well!

Research shows a 4-to-1 ratio of positives to negatives in healthy families. In other words, for every time we confront our kids for negative behavior, there should be four instances of praise, compliments and encouragement. Some days it may be difficult, but our goal is to look for and find the positives.

> **T**hink "Positives".
>
> **B**e *specific* with your praise.
> **A**cknowledge all *progress*.
> **L**et your praise be *enthusiastic*.
> **L**augh and have *fun*.
>
> **P**ut yourself in their shoes. *Empathize*.
> **A**lways be a *role model*.
> **R**emember to promote *team* spirit.
> **E**xpect only what is *reasonable*.
> **N**ever criticize in *public*.
> **T**hink *Process*, not *End Product*.
> ©Darrell J. Burnett, Ph.D.

Be *specific* with your praise

While we're working on keeping a 4-to-1 ratio of positives to negatives, it is especially important to remember to praise specifics. We want our kids to hear positives about themselves. General, vague remarks, such as *good game* or *nice try* are less likely to register than specific remarks, which kids can visualize and remember later. Kids are much more likely to hear and to remember specific remarks such as, "Hey, I was really impressed with your speed. You were really flying down that first-base line on your hits today!", or "You're really getting good at throwing the ball to the right base!", or "You really know how to get your glove down on the ball on those grounders!"

Acknowledge all *progress*

One of the reasons kids get discouraged in T-Ball is because they don't see themselves as getting any better at baseball. They compare themselves to other kids, and it stops being fun. As parents, we can help our kids focus on their progress in any of three areas: *frequency*, *duration* or *intensity*.

Frequency is helping them notice that they're doing something **more often** (hitting the ball out of the infield, stopping a grounder, throwing to the right base, two times compared to one time last game).

Duration is helping them notice that they're doing something for a **longer time** (stopped two grounders in a row, threw to the right base twice in a row). Sometimes, we have to be creative, like the dad who praised his 5-year-old for paying attention to the game for two consecutive batters without picking dandelions while in right field!

Intensity is the amount of **energy expended** (running as hard as possible down the first-base line after hitting the ball off the tee, chasing after a ball in the outfield, cheering loudly for the team, taking as full a swing as possible at bat).

With all these possibilities, no practice or game should go by without our helping our kids notice some progress. And remember, any progress, no matter how small, is still progress.

Let your praise be *enthusiastic*

We want our kids to hear our positives. We increase the likelihood of being heard if we praise with lots of enthusiasm. Kids pay attention to noise. They like action, commotion and emotion. So, when we praise them, we've got to "A.C.E." them, with **A**ction, **C**ommotion and **E**motion. Lots of applause, lots of high fives, lots of cheering.

Unfortunately, we often save our animated emotional reactions for negatives and mistakes. We would do well to monitor our reactions, and keep our enthusiasm and animated responses for positives. Animated praise, coupled with calm reactions to mistakes, will help build confidence in our kids, and allow them to acknowledge their mistakes and learn from them.

Laugh and have *fun*

When you think of the hurried pace of life today, and the pressures faced by youth at increasingly earlier ages, it is all the more imperative that we keep T-Ball as a haven for fun and games. The pressures of growing up hit all too soon. We certainly don't want to add pressure in the entry-level area of recreational sports.

In all the surveys, kids say that "fun" is the No. 1 reason why they play sports. We have to remember to keep fun the focus. Besides, laughter is healthy. It reduces stress, it enhances performance. Kids learn better if they're having fun. If they have fun at this entry level, they'll be back for more.

Put yourself in their shoes — *empathize*

Two of the cornerstones of self-esteem are a sense of feeling *worthwhile* and a sense of *dignity*. It is very difficult for children to feel worthwhile or respected if the adults in their world don't seem to want to take the time to see the world through the eyes of a child.

As adults we sometimes forget that our kids are just kids, not small adults. Sometimes we forget what it was like to be a kid. It's very helpful to make a concerted effort to see the world through the eyes of the T-Baller.

The way we communicate with our T-Ballers, on the field or off, is important. We have to watch our nonverbal messages. We have to remember that an intimidating tone of voice, or threatening finger pointing can be devastating to a fragile young T-Baller. Making comparisons to siblings ("your older sister was hitting the ball to the outfield at your age"; "your older brother knew how to throw the ball straight at your age") only serve to destroy self-esteem. Listening is essential. Listening, with eye contact, while your T-Baller talks about feelings connected with fears of making mistakes, fears of getting hurt, fears of getting made fun of by other players, can bring you much closer to your T-Baller.

We've got to remember what T-Ball is all about for kids. It's about kids learning to play with other kids. It's about kids learning to take turns, to have fun, to learn new skills and to handle mistakes, all the while being buoyed by empathic parents.

Always be a *role model*

As parents, like it or not, our T-Ballers look to us as a model for how to act when it comes to sports. If we want to teach them to have fun and to show good sportsmanship, we have to check our own behavior. The focus should be on *fun* and on the *kids* having fun.

There is simply no place for parents who "lose it" publicly at a T-Ball game. There is no place for parents who publicly challenge a manager or coach about player position, batting order or playing time. There is no place for a parent who publicly berates a volunteer umpire. There is no place for public put-downs, sarcasm or taunting at any recreational sports activity, and especially T-Ball. These public displays of poor sportsmanship not only serve as poor examples, but they embarrass the kids, take away from their concentration, take the spotlight away from the kids and take away from the fun.

We have to monitor our behavior, and we have to monitor the other parents' behavior as well, reminding everyone that the kids are watching. If we, as parents, have complaints about what is going on with our kids, we need to address our complaints in private, rationally, away from the kids. We'll get a lot more accomplished by calmly talking with the manager or coach or board of directors than by yelling threats from the stands. Most parents are fine examples of good sportsmanship. It is important that they set the tone for that small percentage who "lose it."

Remember to promote *team* spirit

The team concept really enhances a kid's sense of **belonging**. As parents, we can do a lot to promote team spirit with our kids. Attending the first team meeting at the beginning of the season, getting to know the other parents, getting to know the other kids, can really get the season off to a great start. Realistically, not all parents are going to blend together, but the atmosphere of togetherness sends a message to the kids.

Parents can get actively involved with coaches and team members in coming up with nicknames for each player and then cheering for each kid by name at the game. It's amazing what it does for kids when they hear another parent recognize them at the game, or at the supermarket. Helping with the team banner, and then displaying it at the game tells the kids that the team is important.

It takes special effort on the part of parents of T-Ballers to get them to start thinking "we" instead of "me". Parents should discourage their kids from criticizing other kids on the team and, of course, they should be aware of their own remarks about the other kids. Singling out a different kid each week for special positive recognition, so that each kid is recognized by the end of the season, also builds the sense of team spirit. Enthusiastic parent participation in team picnics, pizza parties and photos are all opportunities in building a sense of belonging among the kids on the team.

Expect only what is *reasonable*

As our kids start T-Ball, we must remind ourselves to be *realistic* in what we expect. Kids at this age are usually anxious to please adults and look to them for acknowledgment that they have met adult expectations. Likewise, they are easily disappointed in themselves if they don't meet those expectations. Keeping this in mind, it's important for us, as parents, to make sure that what we expect of our T-Ballers is realistic and within their ability to accomplish. Whether it's physical coordination skills, attention span, motivation or dedication, we have to remember that we're dealing with kids at an entry level.

If a kid is not taking a "full cut" with the bat it may be due to coordination skills at the early age, not because the kid is not trying. If a T-Baller spends more time chasing down butterflies than fly balls, it may be due to a short attention span, not because the kid doesn't like baseball. If a T-Baller isn't thrilled about practice drills with us in the backyard, it may be because the youngster at this age is motivated by fun and action, not by dull, boring routine.

We have to remind ourselves that, at the entry-level, the goal is to make sure kids associate T-Ball with having fun. If we're busy telling them how they're not living up to our expectations, it won't be fun for them. The best rule of thumb at the T-Ball level is to praise our kids just for participating, regardless of their skills, attention span, motivation or dedication.

We also have to be realistic in terms of what we expect from the manager or coaches. We can't expect the kids to develop and hone their skills from a short practice and game each week. As parents, we can reinforce what the manager or coach is teaching by practicing the skills with our kids during the week, always in an atmosphere of fun and relaxation.

Never criticize in *public*

T-Ballers will make mistakes. That's how they learn. One lesson that is hopefully learned in T-Ball is that it's OK to make a mistake.

How do we teach a T-Baller that it's OK to make a mistake? The key is our reaction to the mistake. If we yell, scream, humiliate and publicly confront the child when the mistake is made, the danger is that the kid may then become afraid of the reaction, and, out of fear, will avoid making any future mistakes by simply not trying. Or, the kid may become so preoccupied with not making a mistake that he becomes extremely tense and loses concentration, becoming unable to perform.

If we stay calm in our reactions, and if we talk to the child privately, away from the crowd, there's a chance he or she will look at the mistake, learn from it and try again. When giving constructive criticism, the sandwich method is most effective. That is, the negative feedback is sandwiched between two positive remarks.

For example, if a kid lets a grounder go through his legs, instead of repeatedly yelling, "Get down on the ball! Get down on the ball!", we might consider calling our kid aside after the game, and saying something like, "You're really hustling to get over in front of the grounders. I know it's hard to remember to bend down when that ball is coming at you on the ground. We'll have to work with you on getting your glove down on the ground when the ball comes. Maybe you could practice rubbing the glove on the ground to make sure the glove is down there when the ball comes. We can practice that this week. I really liked the way you hustled after the ball to get it back to the pitcher."

Remember, dignity, being treated with respect, is a cornerstone of self-esteem. No T-Baller, or any child, for that matter, deserves to be publicly berated or humiliated.

Think *process*, not *end product*

Finally, part of getting into our kids' T-Ball world is realizing that they're more into *process*, while we as adults are more into *end products*. When an adult sees a kid coming off the field after a game, the typical questions are, "Who won? What was the score? Did you get any hits?" But when you hear little kids talking to each other you hear things like, "Did you see their cool uniforms?", or "Did you see that turtle out in left field?", or "Your mom always brings the best snacks!"

If we stay focused on end products, we're bound to be disappointed that our T-Ballers aren't achieving the goals which we have set for them. But, if we see each event in the context of a total process as they move through their T-Ball experiences, we'll help avoid our disappointing looks and remarks, and we'll stay focused on the fun and enjoyment of T-Ball. In fact, as we participate in the entry level with our kids, we would do well to put everything in perspective. T-Ball is the beginning of a process which will take our kids through the various levels of skills and involvement in youth sports. Hopefully, we can keep our kids involved in the process over the years. Hopefully, by keeping our focus on helping them experience the fun of T-Ball, at the end of the season, regardless of skill development, we will have contributed to getting them to where they want to come back next year to continue the process of developing skills, learning to feel self-confident, and, above all, having fun playing ball.

Dr. Burnett is a clinical and sport psychologist, a dad and a youth sports coach. He has worked with children and families for more than 20 years and is a published authority in positive parenting. In addition to many booklets, audio tapes and other materials, he is the author of Youth, Sports & Self Esteem: A Guide for Parents *(Masters Press).*

This Game is Fun

Mike Veeck, St. Paul Saints

There is in a world that is increasingly confusing a simple game known as baseball. In a world of infinite possibilities and situations,

baseball is one of the few things I know that's finite. In the pages of this book, you will learn the rules to this wonderful game. You will learn ways to make it more enjoyable. Parents, more importantly, will learn how to participate with their children, in one of the true rights of passage. If we are really successful, they will recapture a feeling from a time they'll tell you about. Baseball is a dance, a form of communication ... in short, universal. Whether you are a boy or a girl, man or woman, uncle or aunt, or grandparent, it is impossible to escape the hours of joy one can share huddled around a diamond. No matter the level, watching someone you love participate adds immeasurably to the pleasure of baseball.

For me, the game connects me to a grandparent that I never met. It reminds me of the wonderful hours whiled away playing catch with my dad on the Eastern Shore of Maryland. Talking with my mom, subjecting her to hours and hours of what ifs, whys and wherefores of a game that seemed as physical as ballet and as mystical. Heroes are still in vogue in baseball. All of these things ring true because of the basic tenant of the game: baseball is a game and fun is good. It should be approached at any age with reckless and carefree abandon. It doesn't need a lot of rules. It needs even less skill. It's a fairly simple game. You throw the ball, you hit the ball, you run. Would that all of life could be that carefree! And maybe it can. Fun is good! It's the number one creed here at the St. Paul

Saints. Baseball is fun, and because of that, it's easy to take the next step.

Baseball is good. Embrace the game. Play it to enhance and increase your capabilities, but most importantly, play it for fun. Play it with your heart over your head and with passion. At the end of the day, it is important who won, but it doesn't much matter if it was you or the other team. What really matters is that it was fun. Go for it! Carry the gospel and let the sound of laughter reverberate off every building and every tree across this wonderful global network, know as the ball yard.

Mr. Veeck, president of the St. Paul Saints, is part of a legendary baseball family, and has proven that the emotions and values of the game can be preserved, regenerated — even enhanced — with proper attention and purpose.

T-Ball: Whose Game is it, Anyway?

Dr. Elliot Johnson, Winning Run Foundation

Approximately 20 million children between the ages of 6 and 18 participate in nonschool-sponsored youth sports programs. These programs, including T-Ball, have potential to bring great physical and psychological benefit to youngsters. Conversely, they can also bring disillusionment and frustration to parents, coaches and kids.

What determines whether the experience of youth sports participation is positive or negative? The value of each program depends upon how it is coached and administered. The benefits gained depend upon the insights of coaches and parents as they provide the environment that is conducive to the physical, emotional, social and spiritual development of each child. The purpose of this section is to add to those insights in the hope of making a good idea — T-Ball — an even greater experience for all concerned!

Why Kids Play and Coaches Coach

Numerous studies have been conducted to determine why kids play youth sports. Though results vary somewhat at different age levels, certain generalizations can be drawn. The No. 1 reason young children play sports is to have fun. Children have a "play urge" and sports are designed to be fun. Sports satisfy that intrinsic urge for physical expression.

Secondly, kids play sports to be with friends. It seems that at a young age we realize that experiences are more fun when they are shared! We really do need others!

Third, research shows that kids play sports to learn skills. They want to feel successful, to feel they have accomplished something worthwhile.

Fourth, kids play for the excitement of the sport. The risk-taking of sports participation is stimulating to humans, even at young ages. The fun of being on a team, to improve their skills and the thrill of the game motivate kids to play. On the other hand, winning games, awards or championships consistently rank as lower priorities for youth sport participants.

The question must be asked: Do kids play for the same reasons that youth sport coaches coach?

The answer to this question varies. T•BALL USA is committed to learning, teamwork and fun. These motives should energize all coaches of very young children. But across the country, some programs lose sight of valid reasons for youth sports. Volunteer coaches who are trained by televised pro sports or by their own warped, frustrated experiences as athletes sometimes think they are the reincarnation of Vince Lombardi. City championships, trophies and all-star teams can blur the intrinsic message of youth sports. It's up to parents and coaches to send the right message to kids: Have fun and — win or lose — you are a worthwhile person!

Characteristics of Preadolescents

Between the ages of 2 and 5, children develop proficiency in running, jumping, hopping, galloping, skipping, climbing, balancing, throwing and catching. There is little difference between boys and girls in size and body composition at these ages. These children have short attention spans, are eager to please adults and are beginning to develop skills of sharing, listening and following directions.

From ages 5 to 11, there remains little gender difference in size and body composition. But there are consistent differences in motor skills, with girls generally demonstrating more flexibility and fine motor coordination and boys achieving higher levels in the standing broad jump, running speed, throwing distance and hand grip strength. Both sexes are developing attitudes concerning authority, adults, competition, responsibility, right and wrong, and rules. Many live in a constant state of flux. Children must learn to handle losing, and it is important for the coach to be more concerned with the development of the individual than with winning games.

Most boys thrive on rough and tumble activities as they become more coordinated at ages 9 to 11. Reaction times are improving and a real growth spurt is just around the corner. Good instruction, strenuous activity, recognition as individuals and chances to appraise themselves are important.

Interests broaden and attention spans lengthen. These kids crave recognition and have a strong sense of rivalry and independence. They enjoy competition, but may become angry or easily discouraged when tired. Confidence building is essential, but the complexities of the game are still incomprehensible to beginners. They may make mistakes and lose poise. They want to hit a pitched fastball but are afraid of being hit! They respond to immediate success or failure, rather than looking at the long-range picture.

Idolization of a sports personality and fantasizing are common. The preadolescent takes booing very personally and may become depressed, break down into tears and withdraw completely. These children need support and help. Parental opinions carry a great deal of weight at this age. Preadolescents want very much to please their parents. Some research suggests that at ages of 7 to 9 years children believe results are based purely upon how hard they have tried. These children don't understand that ability can limit effectiveness. At 9 to 10 years of age, children attribute performance to both ability and effort.

At 11 to 12 years of age, ability and effort are completely differential and the fact that ability level can limit the effect of trying hard is understood. Yet, how many youth sport coaches stop to think about what the children they coach are capable of comprehending?

Sport psychologist Thomas Tutko lists five principles to remember when coaching the preadolescent:

1) Be concerned with the person — not the performance.
2) Understand and attempt to meet the needs of the child.
3) Make athletic participation a positive experience.
4) Protect and support the child in situations he or she is not prepared to handle.
5) Focus on small but meaningful goals, reinforced by rewards.

Values and Hazards of Youth Sports

During the 1970s, historian J.W. Berryman saw the rise of highly organized youth sports programs for children as one of the most significant social trends. Involvement in youth sports guarantees many youngsters who won't be skilled enough to play in high school a chance to play in organized competitive games. Character traits of self-discipline, honesty, leadership, cooperation, aspiration to achieve, courage, persistence, sportsmanship, respect for authority and physical fitness are to be encouraged via youth sports. Much of this encouragement is being given in programs across America.

But in other situations, improperly run programs can breed deceit, hatred, selfishness and violence. As Rainer Martens has warned, "It is the interaction with parents, teammates and coaches that determines if sports help the child to develop morally or immorally."

Youth sports can give families a common interest and perhaps furnish a fatherless son with a father figure in the person of a coach. Or, compulsive volunteer coaches can disrupt family routines, create "youth league widows" and become negative role models. Aiming for worthy goals is a positive character trait, but excessive psychological and physical demands placed upon children by parents and coaches can diminish the spontaneous value of play. It seems that youth want to have fun and learn skills, but a great many drop out when encountering pressure from adults to win. Indeed, the high dropout rate in most sports, estimated to reach 75 percent by age 15, must be addressed.

In some cases adults have increased children's aspirations by exaggerating their talent, thereby substituting extrinsic for intrinsic motivation. When the child is unable to meet the exterior expectations, he becomes frustrated and drops out.

The stated objectives of T•BALL USA are consistent with sound educational philosophy. Since most kids have forgotten the score before they reach the concession stand anyway, there is no need for league championships in this entry-level sport. Everyone plays and everyone hits the stationary ball. The emphasis is on hitting, learning to run bases in the correct sequence and at the proper time, catching, throwing, teamwork and fun — with emphasis on the latter!

Helpful hints for parents and coaches

1) Never overload a player with too much information at once. The mind can only focus on one thing at a time.

2) Remove pressure by using positive reinforcement. It usually works much better than punishment. After all, no one strikes out or makes an error on purpose.

3) Treat each player as a unique individual. Not everyone has the same problem in learning the skills and many are atypical.

4) Make sure players have fun. Have fun yourself, and project that impression. If kids don't enjoy youth sports, it's pretty hard to justify them!

5) Be tolerant and patient. Kids won't perform perfectly, nor will you coach perfectly. Each person is of equal value, no matter what his skill level.

6) Set a good example by your behavior. Kids need positive role models and adults have much responsibility to set a good example.

7) Young players are not miniature adults. It takes time for them to grow and mature. Saturation with fundamentals and drills cannot replace maturation of their young bodies!

8) Be honest with kids, but encouraging at the same time. Kids can spot phoniness a mile away!

9) Self-image is critical to success. Build self-concept by setting achievable goals with kids. People will never be all they can be until they feel good about themselves.

10) Most young people value parents' opinions more than anyone else's. They want to please both parents and coaches. Therefore, parents and coaches must work together!

11) How you say something is as important as what you say. Fear, intimidation, sarcasm and ridicule are not valid means of motivation in youth sports.

12) Correct players when they are most receptive. Most players are least receptive to correction immediately after a crucial mistake in a game.

13) Players compete with opponents as well as against them. We need our opponents, for the competition makes both individuals better. Real character never sulks nor taunts an opponent. Aggression is great, but never hostility and hatred.

14) Make a friend of a kid. If you do, you'll have a friend for life.

15) Don't blame officials for a bad judgment call. If you do, and you allow kids to blame others, you do them a real disservice and their improvement will be much less. Respect authorities, for without them there would be no game!

16) Most people feel insecure in some ways . . .including in sports. Build security into children and they will perform better.

17) Instruct wisely. Telling someone he did wrong without telling him how to do it properly makes him afraid to try again.

18) Remember, being on a less-skilled team doesn't make one a loser!

Don't Forget the Juice!

As my two sons progressed through the levels of youth sports (football, basketball and baseball) to become college athletes, I have become ever more firmly convinced that the games exist for the participants. Kids' games aren't for volunteer coaches to improve their status in the community as hard-driving winners. The games are not for parents to vicariously relive their "glory days" through their children, or to expect their offspring to fulfill all their own failed fantasies. The most enlightening feature I can recall from years of observing youth contests is that of kids making a beeline for the refreshments where the coach paid for the soft drinks after the game! Yet, I've also observed a burly youth coach jerk a kid up to his eye level and chew him out like he had committed the unpardonable sin on the practice field. It wasn't a pretty sight.

The values of youth sports depend upon how they are coached. Parents and coaches have a great responsibility to see that kid's games are played for the purposes of skill development, social interaction, emotional growth — and fun!

Dr. Johnson is founder and executive director of The Winning Run Foundation, a nonprofit organization that publishes athletic-related materials, runs baseball camps and clinics, gives sports seminars and provides speakers. Author of many sports books and two videos, he is a college baseball coach and father of two players.

Safety and Health

Dr. Letha Griffin, Peachtree Orthopedic Clinic

Participation in T-Ball gives children the opportunity to learn teamwork while improving physical fitness, developing coordination and learning self-discipline and sportsmanship. Yet, T-Ball, like other sport activities, does expose children to some risk of injury. Not surprisingly, the injury risk in organized sports such as T-Ball has been reported to be one-half to one-third that which occurs in unorganized or informal play activities.*

To further decrease this injury risk, parents of youngsters who play T-ball should be encouraged to:

■ Select a sports program for their children in which the coaches are caring and knowledgeable, and one in which the coaches and management communicate well with both children and their parents. Other parents in the community are typically an excellent referral source, or one could ask about programs sponsored by park and recreation departments or your local YMCA. Make certain that the program you select stresses good sportsmanship and rule enforcement. Injury rates decrease when rules of the sport are enforced.

■ Purchase approved and appropriately sized protective equipment for their children. "Hand-me-downs" are fine as long as they fit properly and are in good repair. Shoes for T-Ball should have multiple rubber cleats. Metal cleats are dangerous and smooth-bottomed shoes do not provide enough traction. Shoestrings should be an appropriate length, in good repair, and tied so they will not come untied during a game and cause a youngster to trip. Catchers must have a mask, helmet, chest protector with collar, and throat and shin guards. Often, the catcher's equipment is provided by the organization. If so, be careful that if a child is smaller or larger than the average child of that same age group, that the equipment is adaptable. If not, the parents may wish to purchase or borrow safety equipment for their child, since safety equipment that is too big or too small provides a false sense of protection.

■ Insist that children tuck in their shirts during play so that another player's finger won't be caught in a jersey hemline and hyperextended. Jewelry — watches, rings, chains and earrings — should be removed. If an earring is caught on a piece of clothing or by the ball, it can literally rip through the end of the ear lobe. A ring caught in clothing can strip the skin from a finger.

■ Help their young children get in condition for sports just as older children and adults do. Growing bodies should be balanced bodies, and therefore, all muscle groups need to be developed equally. An easy way to do this is to encourage children to participate in a variety of sport activities during their growth years; that is, have them swim, bike, walk, hike, or run as well as play T-ball and other group sports. Too often children are driven to school and sport, and therefore do not get the conditioning advantage of biking, walking or running during normal activities of daily living.

■ Explain the benefits of warming up and stretching before play. It is a myth that all children are flexible. In fact, during times of rapid growth, if bones grow faster than the muscles around them, these tight muscles pulling on bones can cause irritation to the bone's growth centers, resulting in overuse injuries. An example of such an overuse injury is heel pain in young children caused by a tight Achilles tendon irritating the growth center of the heel bone. A child with Sever's disease, as this entity is known, will complain of heel pain and tends to run and walk on his toes in an attempt to decrease the stress of the tight tendon on the heel bone. Rest relieves the pain, and this, combined with proper stretches for the calf muscles and their Achilles tendon, will typically resolve the problem. However, it is also better to prevent such injuries by properly stretching rather than treating them after they occur.

■ Get children to practice and play on time so that they are not rushed but have time to warm up and mentally focus on playing ball before the game or practice begins. Frequently, injuries occur because children are late and in a hurry, and therefore are not careful.

■ Instruct children in principles of good nutrition since good nutrition is a must — not just for the pregame meal but every meal. Diets should be approximately 60 percent carbohydrates, 25 percent fat and 15 percent protein, with the selection of foods balanced between the food groups as suggested by the U.S. Agricultural Association (Fig. 1). Snacks eaten 1-2 hours before play may provide needed energy. Excellent sources of immediate energy are foods high in carbohydrates and low in fats, like crackers, muffins, bagels, bananas, apples, toast and jelly, or yogurt. Have youngsters drink water before, during and after games, especially in hot weather. Encourage them to drink water even if they are not thirsty. Typically, the thirst reflex is not triggered until one percent of the body weight has been lost in sweat. Young children may be more likely to drink if the water is flavored. Substituting diluted juice, commercial sports beverages or a similar product for water may be beneficial.

■ Make certain children are well-rested for games and practices. Sleepovers are fun, but sleep is essential the night before a game. The amount of sleep each child needs may vary slightly. Therefore, while some children may be able to stay up until 10 or 11 p.m. the night before a game, your child may need to be in bed by 9 p.m., especially if he or she is an early riser. Tired children, like tired adults,

Figure 1: Food Pyramid

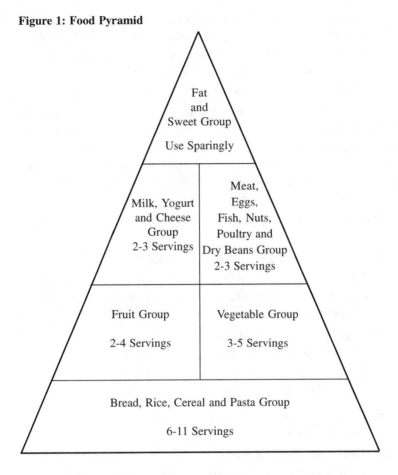

are not as alert as they need to be, and therefore more injury prone.

■ Volunteer to help maintain and "police" the field of play to make certain all holes are filled and all litter is removed. Ankle injuries frequently occur when a youngster steps into a hole while running. A piece of glass or a bottle top left in the grass can cut a player who is sliding.

■ Stress that sports and fitness are FUN! Don't directly or indirectly put demands on children which make them feel stressed. Not only is such stress bad from a psychological standpoint, but when one feels stressed to succeed or not let another down, attention often is not as acutely focused on the activity of the moment nor are reflexes as quick to respond as they may need to be to avoid injury.

Remember, T-ball is not only a time for youngsters to learn the fundamentals of baseball, while gaining an appreciation of the rules of the sport and the importance of following these rules, but it is also a time to develop a love of this sport in particular, and hopefully a love of all sport in general. Sport participation encourages fitness, and fitness is essential for good health.

Safety tips for children are similar to those for parents and include:

- Play fairly. Follow the rules of the sport.
- Maintain your safety equipment. Always bring it to games and practices, and make certain the equipment is fastened securely to you so that it won't loosen and slip.
- Bring your water bottle to games and practices, and drink often, even if you don't feel thirsty.
- Tuck in your shirt, tie your shoes securely and remove all jewelry before you play.
- Go to bed on time before games and practices. You can't play well or safely when tired.
- Get to the field in plenty of time before practices and games so that you have time to warm up and stretch.
- Condition for your sport by biking, swimming, or walking with your parents or friends. You can lift weights like your dad, mom, or older brother or sister if you use light weights with a number of repetitions rather than heavy weights with few repetitions. Remember, free weights are usually better for you to use than machines since most weight machines are not adaptable to young children with smaller bones. Always ask dad, mom, your coach, or a knowledgeable teenager or other adult about the proper

form to use when doing your lifts, as well as other tips they may have on weight training in general.

Coaches of young children just beginning their sport career are in a very influential position. Their attitude toward sport will help to shape the attitude of the youngsters they coach. Coaches can make sports safe and fun by:

- Insisting that all children arrive on time to practices and games, dressed appropriately with jewelry off, shoes tied tightly and water bottles in hand.

- Encouraging frequent water breaks during practices and taking a water "toast" between innings of play.

- Establishing early in the youngster's sports' career the importance of listening to the coach and following the rules of the game. Trying to trip, or otherwise injure an opposing team member should never be tolerated.

- Being positive in their instruction to children, as confident players are less frequently injured than timid, hesitant players.

- Never permitting children to play when they are injured or sick. Alert parents if you suspect that a child is hurt; for example, if you see a player limping while running bases, make certain that the parents know that the child is having a problem.

- Removing injured players from the game and helping them to ice and elevate the injured part until medical help is available.

- Noting the location of the phone nearest to the playing field, and always having a quarter to use this phone in case an emergency occurs and help must be summoned. Be certain to know if any team member has a medical problem that might result in a medical emergency during play and be prepared for such emergencies. For example, if a child is asthmatic, diabetic or has severe allergic reactions to bee or wasp stings, ask the parents what to do if the child develops such a reaction. Better yet, encourage the youngster's parents to always be at games and practices. Medical crises can be minimized if a treatment or response plan has been established ahead of time.

■ Being familiar with stretching and conditioning exercises that are appropriate for the age group you are coaching, and incorporating these into practices and pregame, warm-up activities.

■ Having a group meeting with your players and their parents at the beginning of the season to discuss equipment needs, the importance of following the rules and of good sportsmanship, the advantage of proper stretching, conditioning, and adequate rest as well as to review principles of good nutrition.

■ Policing the fields before games or practices or establish a team or parent squad to do this.

Remember, you are a key figure. The attitude of the players and their parents will, to a very large extent, be shaped by what you say and do. Be a positive influence. Help ensure safety in kids' sports.

———————————

Dr. Griffin is a specialist in sports medicine, and knee and arthroscopic surgery at the Peachtree Orthopaedic Clinic in Atlanta, Ga. She is an authority on safety for young children entering sports and has spoken on this subject on Good Morning America.

* As reported by the U.S. Consumer Product Safety Commission in the *Play It Safe* brochure published by the American Academy of Orthopaedic Surgeons, 1995, Rosemont, Ill.

A Model Instructional Program
Richard Blalock, Diamond Sports Park

Diamond Sports Park in Gainesville, Fla., has developed a highly successful program based on quality teaching, an innovative rotation system for skills training and a noncompetitive playing environment. Games are designed to focus on the basic fundamentals. Richard Blalock, the park's sports director, writes:

The T-Ball Program at Diamond Sports Park is designed to be a purely instructional program for boys and girls ages 5 and 6. So often T-Ball programs start out with intentions of being noncompetitive, but when the adults get involved, things tend to become competitive between the adults and the children are caught in the middle. Another problem that we have seen is one team may have a coach that has more experience than the other coaches and those children advance at a faster rate than the others.

In an attempt to insure that adult egos do not get involved and that all children receive the same quality of instruction, we hire as instructors college students majoring in sports administration, physical education, recreation or any other related fields. By hiring the instructors we can insure that the program is consistent. One other important consideration when hiring our instructors is that we hire at least one female instructor for the program. We have found that children of this age are so used to being with "mom" that they feel more comfortable, as do the parents, being consoled by a female instructor when they are physically hurt or have their feelings hurt.

The next step is to certify the instructors through the National Youth Sports Coaches Association. We then give them a notebook that has a description of all of the skills and drills that will be used as well as a log of which will be used at each practice. The instructors choose what station they will instruct for each practice and they are responsible for the proper instruction at that station.

When the instructors are squared away, we form the teams and schedule games and practices. Teams are split into groups of six and games and practices are scheduled on Monday and Friday. The parents receive a schedule that indicates which days are games and which days are practices as well as what skill stations will be taught at practice. The parents appreciate knowing that the schedule is consistent throughout the season so that they can incorporate it into their plans.

Practices are set up more like clinics. Four skill stations are established. A group of 12 children spends 30 minutes at each station and rotates through the skill stations at each practice. By using the skill stations, each child is given the same instruction and advances at the same rate.

Games are played with three teams. Team "A" bats, Team "B" plays the right side of the field (pitcher, first base, second base, right field and right-center) and Team "C" plays the left side of the field (catcher, shortstop, third base, left field and left-center). Team "A" bats through three times then rotates to the right side of the field. Team "B" rotates to the left side of the field (the children playing the outfield rotate to the infield as the children playing the infield rotate to the outfield). Team "C" comes to bat. This allows each child to bat three times in a short period of time and play two positions per game. But more importantly, it keeps the child's attention during the game because he or she is constantly moving. Each game stresses a phase or skill of the game. Each game builds to a total basic understanding of the game and prepares for the next step.

The league ends with a family day cookout. Each family brings a food item and we provide the individual awards. The children are divided into four teams. Two teams are made up of the children moving up to the next age division and they play a three-inning game. Two teams are made up of the children that are returning to the T-Ball program and they play a three-inning game. The parents are involved in the actual coaching of the teams. This is a day in which the entire family is involved and the parents can see the progression that their child has made.

Mr. Blalock is sports director for Diamond Sports Park in Gainesville, Fla., which has developed a highly successful program based on quality teaching, an innovative rotation system and a noncompetitive playing situation with focus on basic fundamentals.

Keeping the Fun in T-Ball
Dr. Deborah Bright

T-Ball is your child's first organized team sport, and for him or her it means fun. Your active involvement in this activity can enhance that fun ... or take some of it away. Here are a few guidelines to help keep the fun in the game.

■ **Pay attention to *signals***

During games or practice rounds, we often try to send our children *signals* using various facial expressions. Be aware of those expressions, and make sure that the message you are sending isn't one of disappointment, rejection or anger. Your child will be singling you out in the crowd, looking for cues to indicate whether you are pleased. Frowns on faces and angry looks send messages that hamper self-confidence and spoil the fun.

■ **Help with disappointments**

Winning and losing is not the primary focus of the sport at this level. What's more important is learning how to play the game, developing skills and having fun. No one likes not doing well — at any age. If you listen to your child express his or her disappointment at the end of a game, that's enough. There's no need for big lectures on "understanding life" and "how to recover from failures" . . . rather, just listening and understanding what your child is feeling at the moment is plenty, with maybe a quick reminder about the importance of learning. At this age, within 10 minutes, your son or daughter will have forgotten the disappointments and be moving on to something else.

■ A word of caution about older siblings

If your child has older brothers or sisters who are also involved in sports, be careful about making comparisons. Again, at their age, they want to please you, and if they are reminded of how you admire the accomplishments of their older brothers and sisters, they may come to think that you expect the same of them.

Be very careful when making comparisons, and if necessary, have a talk with your child and explain just how you feel.

■ Join in the fun!

Play with your son or daughter. Besides teaching specific motor skills, you can throw in a few mental skills to help ensure that the sport remains fun while fine-tuning your child's physical abilities. These mental skills are referred to as *Quick Charges* — techniques to help stay at your best in high-pressured situations.

Here's a good *Quick Charge* to use to help your child get rid of negative thoughts. When your child is upset for not coming through for the team, rather than say "Don't let it bother you, just stay in the game," throw in the *Blackboard Quick Charge*.

- It's practiced by first envisioning a blackboard, then writing on it all the negative things going through your mind.

- Once you have the list on the board, imagine taking a giant eraser and wiping the blackboard clean.

- Finally, imagine writing on the clean blackboard what you need to concentrate on next.

Or, to help minimize pregame jitters, teach your child to use the *Untying Stomach Knots Quick Charge*.

- When a knot forms in your child's stomach, tell him or her:

- Inhale and tighten the muscles in your stomach and hold them that way for a few moments (practice this part of the Quick Charge by making believe you are going to tickle them; they'll catch on!).

- Next, relax the muscles by imagining your stomach being coated with a smooth, cool layer of ice cream. After a few tries, the knots will untie themselves.

There are many Quick Charges that can be used in high-pressure situations. We've only introduced a few to help get your son or daughter off to a good start. As you continue to work with your child, you may come up with some of your own. Passing along these Quick Charges will help your child learn to work well with him or herself, and play at his or her best. Remember, however, that the most important thing you can do as a parent, considering the age of your child, is to keep "fun" in the game. By helping to keep the game fun, you are laying the foundation for your son or daughter to enjoy sports for many years to come.

Dr. Bright, a member of the faculty at New York University, is founder and president of Bright Enterprises, whose sole mission is the design of human technologies for improved performance. Building on a sports background as a ranked woman diver, she is a recognized expert on stress and has worked with professionals in tennis, football and golf to effectively compete in pressure situations.

Developmental T-Ball

Mel Carpenter

Dear Parents:

Developmental T-Ball can be a wonderful experience. We'd like to suggest some guidelines that will help it become just that for you and your child.

- Don't expect too much. Your child may not be able to hit the ball, catch or throw for an out. Always let your child know at the end of each practice or game regardless of ability, that he or she is the No. 1 BEST PLAYER!!!

- Encourage your child and teammates to set a good example by applauding the children on the opposing team.

- Find positive things to say.

- Never make derogatory remarks to players, coaches or parents! All coaching questions or complaints should be made in private, away from the players.

- Always check your own equipment to be sure it is clearly marked with the player's name.

- Remind your child to pay close attention to the coach.

- Remember, T-Ball is designed for your child to learn the basic techniques of baseball and to have FUN! T-Ball is not designed to be a competitive sport. No scores are kept and each player will bat and field.

Hints for the Parents

- Help your player get to the diamond at least 10 minutes before practices and games.

- Remember that your child is excited about the game.

■ Remind the player to listen to the advise of the coach.

■ Do not help your player make excuses about poor play or losing.

■ Every child should be encouraged to give 100 percent of his or her ability. Encouragement, rather than critical remarks, works better with most children.

■ Some of the problems that only you, parent and coach, will be able to solve are:

  • The player finding excuses for losing.

  • The player blaming other players for the loss.

  • The player becoming discouraged with losing.

  • The player losing enthusiasm for the game.

  • The player not enjoying playing the game.

Purpose

T-Ball provides an opportunity for boys and girls to actively participate in playing baseball under conditions favorable for their age. It is designed to teach the following skills:

■ Swinging a bat properly at the ball.

■ Fielding the ball properly.

■ Throwing the ball.

■ Learning and practicing the game of baseball.

Each child will have the thrill of hitting the ball and running the bases. We hope the whole family will be involved in this true spirit of sportsmanship.

HAVE FUN!!!

Mr. Carpenter is the Youth Sports Director for the award-winning Johnson County Park & Recreation District in Shawnee Mission, Kan. The above outline is one of many information communications sent to all concerned with the T-Ball program.

How to Keep Your C.O.O.L. at the Ballpark

Lou Makarowski, Ph.D.

Parents, please pause before you scream too loudly at your children's T-Ball games. Easier said than done? I know; I've crossed the line that divides support and poor taste myself. I know how easy it is to get emotionally involved when you see your child being treated unfairly. But please, try to remember that disorderly parents ruin T-Ball for their kids.

Kids (and parents) just beginning to participate in team sports need to focus on having fun, learning about sportsmanship and the fundamental skills needed to enjoy the game. Adults berating coaches, attacking officials or arguing among themselves frighten and distract the children. Young children are confused and sometimes terrified by adult hostility. This is especially true when parents blow up at a T-Ball game that the family is attending for the purpose of having fun. There is help for parents with hair-trigger tempers. Yes, you can learn how to keep your C.O.O.L. at the ballpark.

To keep your C.O.O.L. at the ballpark, I believe that you must:

C — Consider the context and CONSEQUENCES of your reactions to provocative situations that trigger your anger.

O — Observe your breathing, body tension and communication (self-talk, words and body language) objectively.

O — Organize your options for successful problem solving when provoked.

L — Look to the future, learn from the past and live in the present.

If you are struggling to control your temper during your child's sporting events and would like to change that pattern of behavior, the first step is to consider the *consequences*. You can do this by increasing your awareness of how your behavior affects your child. Some of the consequences your children experience include feeling nervous, embarrassed or ashamed when they hear others criticize your disorderly behavior behind your back.

Ask yourself some questions. Do I really want my child to have to defend me? Kids can be cruel.

Even at 4 or 5 years old, your children will try to defend you or feel guilty for not doing so. Think about it. Think about the pressure you are putting on your child. See your child trying to explain your behavior to others. The pressure of shrugging off or confronting teammates who criticize mom or dad will dull their enthusiasm for T-Ball in particular and competition in general. Remember, youth sports are competitive events. Your outbursts provide grist for the ballpark gossip mill. Rivals may use your behavior to rattle your child. Instead of feeling supported, your child may become the target for teammates' catty remarks. Teammates and parents notice those who consistently display poor sportsmanship. They will comment. If your child is not among the most popular, the comments will not be kind. If you know you have a problem with your temper:

- **Consider the context** as well as the consequences of your reactions to provocative situations that trigger your anger. Is your temper tantrum related to stress that you feel which is originating from some other corner of your life? Work stress? Stress from unrealistic expectations? Develop a plan to deal with your anger *before* you get to the ballfield. Have a talk with your child. Ask how it makes him or her feel to have you yelling "support" from the stands. Listen carefully to what your child tells you. On your way to the event, remind yourself that disorderly behavior *is* poor sportsmanship.

- **Observe your breathing, muscle tension and communication** during the games and practices. If you find yourself tensing up, plan to take a deep breath, and make sure you exhale completely. Scan your body for muscle tension and release it. Be mindful of your self-talk. Your thoughts often trigger angry outbursts. Remind yourself that, "We are here to have a good time. T-Ball is all about building happy memories, making friends and having fun. I don't want my child to have to defend me. The last thing I want to do is embarrass or worry my child."

■ **Organize your options for successful problem solving when provoked**. Check your TEMPERature often. Before it boils over, remember to move slower, talk more softly and bring your funny bone to the ballpark. If necessary, plan to leave the stands and get a soft drink should you find yourself getting too angry.

■ **Look to the future, learn from the past and live in the present**. Visualize yourself as a paragon of sportsmanship. Be on the lookout for other parents who seem to be good role models for civility. You learn a lot by observing and imitating their words and actions. Review your worst flare-ups from the past before and during the game. They will remind you of what *not* to do in the future. Enjoy the outing regardless of the outcome. After all, we still call it a ballgame. Children play games to have fun.

Don't wait until you are out of control. Poor sportsmanship is not productive for anyone. Maybe this year we can avoid some of last year's ugly incidents. Think proactively. A positive plan to keep your C.O.O.L. will stop trouble before it starts. I know it will help your children by providing them with positive role models for fielding tension, anger and other strong emotions. It may even prevent a parent, referee, coach or player from getting hurt in a furor over a bad call.

The purpose of organized youth sports is to provide safe, wholesome recreation for children, certainly not the development of competitive spirit. Why? Perhaps a review of some basic child development information might provide some perspective to this business of competition in youth sports. T-Ball age children have not developed cognitively to the point where they can appreciate the nature of championship or competition. Developmental psychologists tell us that these children do not think abstractly.

Five-year-old youngsters live in the here and now, the present.

Abstract concepts such as competition, championships and making the first team cut are totally foreign to them. Foreign unless they are imitating the adult emphasis they can see and feel. They may mimic the goals of the adults involved in T-Ball competition, but the children certainly don't appreciate the nature of competition. The ability to appreciate competition in the adult sense is delayed until the child's intelligence is developed to the point that they can appreciate abstract concepts.

Think about it! If children still believe in Santa Claus and the Easter Bunny, do you think that they can fully distinguish fantasy from reality? Do you think they can truly appreciate the emotional nature of a competition? Hardly! These children simply believe that they were good or bad depending on whether they pleased or displeased the adults involved.

Children want to love and be loved. When adults are pleased with them, children feel loved and believe they are good. When adults are displeased with them, children feel unloved and believe they are bad. We don't want 5-year-olds who make a mistake, don't earn a starting position or fail to win championships to think they are bad. Do we? Of course not. So let's increase the fun and cut down on the competition in T-ball. This will help you keep your C.O.O.L.

We love our children and want what's best for them. At times we want what's best too much. At times we lose our C.O.O.L. Adult anger scares children, even if the adults are arguing with other adults. Scaring kids isn't the objective of T-Ball.

Dr. Makarowski, author of How To Keep Your C.O.O.L. With Your Kids, *is a family psychologist, peak performance consultant and seminar leader. He is a member of the United States Olympic Committee Sports Psychology Registry and his popular column,* Tips for Success in Sports and Life©, *is nationally syndicated.*

The Game in its Proper Context
Major Robert A. Doss, USMC

The problem with some coaches is not that they take the game too seriously; the problem is that they take the game out of context — they lose their perspective. Kids place a premium on what their coaches emphasize. At the end of a (losing) game, we emphasized appreciating the skill with which the other team had played, and the fact that our kids played hard and had fun. However, after the game, a parent approached me and told me that one of our parents in the bleachers had been making a fuss over our team's lack of success. I phoned the parent and asked him if there was something we needed to talk about and, after a while, we got down to it. He said that he was tired of being humiliated and he was tired of seeing his kid humiliated.

I didn't pull any punches. I told him that if his kid was humiliated, it was because his father was making too much of these games. We had a team that was not good enough to beat good teams. Nothing we did at practice and nothing I said at the game was going to change that.

However, it turned out that the last four games of the season were against teams nearer to our caliber. We won those four games and guess what? The kids were excited about the whole thing. They felt like champions, and we did it without compromising the principles we started with. Unfortunately, there was grumbling in the bleachers again and, of course, I made a second phone call to the same parent I had called earlier. This time his complaint was that he didn't like having his kids play on a team where winning was everything. What do you do?

The point of the anecdote is that whatever you define your season's objectives to be, pursue them aggressively and relentlessly.

If you have a team that will not break out of the bottom ranks of your league, don't press it. Teach them something anyway. I've seen coaches practically give up because they didn't win games. In T-Ball there's always something in which to be successful. If you have a team that can win, try to win. If it can't, teach the players to be good sports or to play hard even when they're losing. Once you figure out what you're going to do, tell the parents and the other coaches and develop a strategy for getting the job done. Once you get going, if you find you need to alter your objectives, have at it. The key point is that you have to take your team's goals seriously, whatever they are, and follow them to the end without taking the game out of context along the way.

©1994. Robert A. Doss Jr.

Major Doss is a Marine pilot. After returning from the Gulf War, he started coaching the way many people do — with a casual comment to a league official about the same dream a lot of parents have of coaching their children on the ballfield. His teams became well-known for their discipline, sense of sportsmanship, competitiveness, skills, and for their ability to play hard and have fun. To help other parents-turned-coaches, Rob has written a book, How To Coach T-Ball Without Going INSANE. *T•BALL USA is delighted to present this excerpt from the book.*

Tee Time

Jerry Waldron, San Diego

For the past 30 years I have had the opportunity of working with children of all ages from preschool to high school seniors. As a recreation leader in the early 1980s at Allied Gardens Recreation Center, I initiated a pilot T-Ball program for children ages 4 and 5.

Besides my love for baseball, I really enjoyed the challenge of teaching such a young group. I had ample equipment: batting tees, and plastic balls and bats, but as I found out, my best resource for success were the parents, and I chose a nice grassy area with few distractions.

The six-week summer program was very successful, primarily due to the parent support which I incorporated from the very beginning. Each child, in order to overcome his or her fears, must feel that he or she can accomplish the task with little chance for failure. The use of the batting tees and the positive encouragement from the instructor and parents allowed the children to learn and have fun at the same time. In this way the parent feels a part of the program as well. Many bought their own tees and helped their children at home.

Each child was put through various T-Ball drills with the help of parents at each station. The equipment was used with small groups at each station. This process provided success which led to the development of an elementary school T-Ball program later that fall.

In 1989, I coached a Little League team. During my practices I had the players hit tennis balls off the tee into the fence, thus conditioning not only the basic mechanics, but hand and eye coordination. After the tee drills they were ready to hit the live pitching off the mound. The team had the highest slugging percentage, which meant the team hit the ball well and got on base the most times.

As a junior high physical education instructor, I teach a unit on softball, and I start everyone on the use of the batting tee. After working on the tees, more seventh-graders have a chance to succeed in hitting the ball and reaching base. By the use of tees and various lead-up activities, I teach the class how to bat an underhand pitch. Here again, confidence is developed with the use of the batting tee. *You must walk before you can run.*

As a high school baseball coach I have implemented the use of batting tees, forcing the players to take time to work on the proper mechanics of hitting through the repetition of hand and eye coordination techniques. In 1984, our high school team won the city baseball championship due in large part to our aggressive batting. Eddie Williams, who currently plays for the major-league San Diego Padres, used the tees extensively and swears they helped him get where he is today.

Today, I use tees as one of my hitting stations at San Diego High School. I sincerely believe their use not only teaches great mechanics, but leads to a self-confidence necessary to be successful.

Remember, positive encouragement, being consistent in all aspects of parental coaching, will help the child to play and remain focused on the task. The simple practice of hitting a ball off a batting tee can lead a child to open up to his or her unlimited potential physically, socially and emotionally.

"Hey, I *can* do it!"

Mr. Waldron is a physical education instructor and varsity baseball coach at San Diego High School. He has been an advocate of the use of a batting tee for all levels of baseball, beginning with the youngest of players.

Young Faces
Tom Stubby

One thing we would like to pass on to all the parents who have young children playing T-Ball is to simply allow the players to have fun. Too many parents expect their kids to improve and become great players before the end of the season. Parents should not focus on the winning or losing aspect of the game. Some parents think that their kids know the score and play to win at this young age. We try to discourage keeping score in our program. We have even asked some players after the game what the score was and they don't know. It is usually the parents or an older sibling who steps in and responds. The score should not be the focus of the game. Let the kids enjoy themselves and get the feel of the game. They will have plenty of time in their sports career to worry about winning and losing. It is not necessary at this time in their lives.

As parents watching the games, you sometimes have to look hard to find that one positive thing your child did well. This positive point is what you and your child can talk about after the game. The first question all parents should ask when their child comes off the field is, "Did you have fun playing today?" It is extremely easy to remember the grounder that was missed or the ball thrown over the fence instead of to first base. Instead of talking about those examples, bring up the time the ball was hit past the infield or a good fielding play.

Maybe your child laid the bat down after hitting the ball instead of throwing it, like quite a few players do at this age. This is an important point to bring up because it is a safety issue. There are many positive aspects of a child's game, if you just make the effort to look.

Watch the players' faces at each game. This is the best part: to see how a young player just lights up after hitting the ball, making a catch or crossing home plate. Even if they are not the one making the play or the hit, the other members of the team will celebrate the success. That is what it's all about — the excitement and the fun of the game. These experiences are what keep kids coming back every season to play again.

For youngsters, little compares with the great feeling that comes from just playing with their friends. It has been proven in several studies that kids enjoy the game and learn more about the game by simply participating. Happiness and joy are all that is needed at a young age; if they made it home or were left on second base really doesn't matter. What counts is that they got on base to start with and did what they felt was correct to them. So the next time your child is running the bases and stops at second instead of continuing, tell your child that he or she did a terrific job making it all the way to second. To see their eyes widen with delight is one of the greatest joys of a parent.

Mr. Stubby is youth sports program director of the West Branch Family YMCA in Omaha, Neb. He believes that the key to success in its 25-year-old program is that there are no bench warmers; beginning with kindergarten, all players field and bat.

National Standards for Youth Sports

To provide youth groups with a focus on what is best for children in their growing, learning years and to enable sport to become a positive experience, 48 leading experts representing a vast variety of disciplines assembled in Washington, D.C. Their goal was to develop standards that all parents should follow. The group studied the role of the parent from the educational, physical, emotional and social aspects of youth sport involvement. Standards were established as a national policy and more than 200 agencies and organizations (including The T•BALL USA Association) have endorsed them. As published by the National Alliance for Youth Sports, the standards initiated "to modify the sports environment for a healthier youth" are:

- Parents must consider and carefully choose the proper environment for their children, including the appropriate age and development for participation, the type of sport, the rules in the sport, the age range of the participants, and the proper level of physical and emotional stress.

- Parents must select youth sports programs that are developed and organized to enhance the emotional, physical, social and educational well-being of children.

- Parents must encourage a drug-, tobacco- and alcohol-free environment for their children.

- Parents must recognize that youth sports are only a small part of a child's life.

- Parents must insist that coaches be trained and certified.

- Parents must make a serious effort to take an active role in the youth sports experience of their children providing

positive support as a spectator, coach, league administrator and/or caring parent.

- Parents must be a positive role model exhibiting sports-
manlike behavior at games, practices and home while giving positive reinforcement to their children and support
to their children's coaches.

- Parents must demonstrate their commitment to their
children's youth sports experience by annually signing a
parental code of ethics.

- Parents, coaches and league administrators must provide
equal sports play opportunity for all youth regardless of
race, creed, sex, economic status or ability.

- Parents as coaches, fans and league administrators must
be drug-, tobacco- and alcohol-free at youth sports activities.

T•BALL USA recognizes that not all leagues have implemented
these standards and that certain elements (such as certified coaches
and ethics code signing) may not be part of local programs for T-
Ball. Nevertheless, the essential qualities of the standards should be
understood for the positive social benefits they will provide to the
child beginning in an organized sports experience.

Recommended reading

Baseball Parent is a newsletter for the parents and coaches
of youth baseball players age 5 and up. Published six times a
year, it features important information to help kids play better.
See the listing in the reference section on page 139.

The Organizations

There are important national and regional groups whose activities and interests include T-Ball. This section will provide statements by and information about associations and representative youth baseball leagues and how they position the sport within their overall programs. Details on where to reach each of these organizations will be found on page 138 in the Reference section of this book.

USA Baseball

USA Baseball is the national governing body of amateur baseball in the United States and a member of the United States Olympic Committee (USOC). The organization selects, trains and supports the USA Baseball teams (senior and junior), which participate in international competitions, including the Olympic Games, Pan Am Games, World University Games and World Championships. USA Baseball became the national governing body of baseball by virtue of the Amateur Sports Act of 1978 and selection by the USOC.

Almost every major national amateur baseball organization in America has been united as a national member of USA Baseball. As a governing organization, USA Baseball strives to coordinate, not duplicate, individual member organizations' programs and projects, so as to provide services unique and essential to amateur baseball. USA Baseball has more than 20 million players, 35 million family members, friends and fans, and 65 national and regional groups as members. An organization of organizations, its national members are the:

Amateur Athletic Union, American Amateur Baseball Congress, American Baseball Coaches Association, American Legion Baseball, Dixie Baseball, Little League Baseball, National Amateur Baseball Federation, National Association of Intercollegiate Athletics, National Baseball Congress, National Collegiate Athletic Association, National Federation of State High School Athletic Associations, National High School Baseball Coaches Association, National Junior College Athletic Association, Police Athletic League, PONY Baseball/Softball and the YMCAs of the USA.

Many of these organizations feature T-Ball as part of their program to introduce young players into the fundamentals of the game. The T•BALL USA Association is also affiliated with USA Baseball and will work with it on programs designed to serve the needs of families with children interested in participating in the sport.

YMCA of the USA

The YMCA is the largest nonprofit community service organization in America. It is at the heart of community life in neighborhoods and towns across the nation. It works to meet the health and social service needs of nearly 15 million men, women and children. Half of all YMCA clientele and staff members are women and half of the users are under 18. Best known for health and fitness (basketball was originated at a YMCA more than 100 years ago) YMCAs teach kids to swim and organize many youth sports programs.

The YMCA states:

We all need a place to belong — a place where we genuinely care about each other; where we pull together for a common cause; where we treat each other with loving kindness, open communications, and support; where we share in decisions. A community. The YMCA nurtures children, supports families and strengthens society. It's a force for hope.

More than 1,500 YMCAs offer T-Ball, baseball and softball. Programs vary by community based on experience and family needs and interest. The North Suburban Family YMCA in Northbrook, Ill., even offers T-Ball to 3-5-year-olds as "an introduction to that great American game — baseball, with instruction in strategy, values and skills. During games, all players learn throwing, catching, batting and different field positions."

The YMCA has been a major factor in the development of T-Ball over the past 40 years and has determined that "the goals of T•BALL USA are very consistent with the YMCA's youth sports philosophy." (See letter to parents, page 3.)

National Recreation and Park Association

The NRPA is a national, nonprofit service organization dedicated to extending the social, health, cultural and economic benefits of parks and recreation. Through its network of 23,000 professionals and civic leaders, NRPA provides programs that help support at-risk youths, resolve crime, encourage healthy lifestyles and create safer communities. Its mission statement is: "To advance parks, recreation and environmental conservation efforts that enhance the quality of life for all people."

Public recreation and parks play a vital role in American life. Local resources are used by 75 percent of the U.S. population (more than 192 million people); 71 percent of Americans live within walking distance of a park, playground or recreation site. Public recreation programs enhance social skills and self-esteem while encouraging constructive use of free time. The use of open space as a sanctuary and of recreation programs as prevention to crime and social unrest amongst are the cornerstone philosophies of NRPA, and have remained so throughout the association's nearly 100 years of service. NRPA stresses the value of "participation" as the primary goal; and the benefits received, such as friendships, teamwork, and the skills that come from playing and interacting with peers result in the development of the strong, resilient character of our youth.

Douglas J. Gaynor, CLP, the president of the NRPA, wrote T•BALL USA:

We are proud to share many of the same philosophical tenets regarding team participation, fitness and the individual growth that comes from participating in recreation and park activities. Many of the sites that are managed by NRPA professionals across the country are indeed home to thousands of organized tee ball league programs and games.

With this type of support and recognition, it is clear that NRPA and T•BALL USA have a great deal in common and will be able to work positively and jointly on a number of projects. We look forward to a continued and mutually beneficial partnership.

Municipal facilities are the most used locations for T-Ball play. Youth baseball leagues, YMCAs, and other service organizations and parent groups schedule their games with the professionals who manage the fields of play.

National Alliance for Youth Sports

The Alliance as a 501-3-C non-profit organization is an advocate for promoting safe and positive sports for America's youth. The Alliance believes that through education and  training of volunteers who administer and coach in organized sports, we can provide a healthy alternative to crime, drugs, violence and other negative influences that young people face today. The Alliance is made up of the following six divisions, each with a unique mission.

The **National Youth Sports Coaches Association** provides training and education to volunteer youth coaches involved in organized out-of-school sports. Its program covers effective coaching techniques, maximizing athletic performance, how to make practices fun and interesting, teaching the basic fundamentals of the sport, the coach as role model, first aid, safety, the psychology of coaching children and many other important aspects. The NYSCA program is available in more than 2,000 community recreation departments and organizations involved with youth activities.

Lifetime Sports & Fitness for Youth
conducts programs for children that help
build the skills and confidence needed to
participate and remain active in sports.
Its Smart Sports Development program
is for parents with children as young as 3 years old to assist
them in developing the skills, such as throwing and catching,
that are needed for organized sports participation.

The **National Institute for Youth Sports Administration** provides
training, education and a variety of
resource materials to assist those responsible for youth sports programming and administration
in public, private and military organizations. Services include videos, books, newsletters and access to the Alliance's
various programs.

The **National Clearinghouse for Youth Sports Information** provides
the public with access to a variety
of information pertaining to youth sports. Its resource library
includes research, books, pamphlets, instructional videos and
other assorted publications and surveys on such subjects as
parental attitudes, youth sport coach certification/training and
sports medicine use among children.

The **National Association of Youth Leagues** is focused on making sports safe and positive through the implementation of the  National Child Protection Program for Youth Sports. Information available through this program enables volunteer and professional youth sports directors the opportunity to understand and identify child abuse in youth sports, and provides volunteer screening procedures and parental education material. Assistance is available to leagues through a wide range of information and services ranging from legal advice to tips on volunteer recruitment.

The **National Youth Sports Officials Association** assists youth leagues and programs in developing quality sports officials. Competent officiating is a necessity, yet many times youth leagues must enlist volunteers to fulfill this vital role. The NYSOA program develops basic skills, teaches fundamentals and encourages beginning officials to have fun despite the pressure to perform well. A variety of educational materials including books, videos and audiocassettes are available from the association.

Little League Baseball, Inc.

Founded in 1939, this nonprofit membership organization is recognized throughout the world for its fostering of the sport and the development of young athletes in both skills and understanding of the game. Teamwork, fair play and citizenship are essential elements of this youth service program. Administered by a professional staff, the national headquarters charters local league units to provide team play programs under well-defined regulations within community/territory limits of not more than 20,000.

T-Ball is the first stage in Little League play. August 1 is the date that determines "league age." Any child who turns 6 before that date can play through ages 7 and 8.

Little League headquarters has established regulations and suggested procedures for T-Ball (essentially, modifications from their Minor League competition for ages 8 - 12) which may be adjusted for individual programs.

Little League has provided T•BALL USA with the following statement:

The Little League Tee Ball program is a training process by which youngsters can learn, develop and practice fundamental baseball and softball skills at an early age and receive maximum enjoyment from the experience. Conventional baseball and softball require that a pitcher throw accurately across home plate within each batter's defined strike zone. Most youngsters 5, 6, 7 and 8 years old have not developed skills to pitch accurately nor to hit a pitched ball. Consequently, neither the batters nor fielders are given ample opportunity to develop fundamental hitting or defensive skills outside an organized Tee Ball program.

The young player benefits in several ways hitting the ball from a prescribed tee. The youngster has the opportunity to develop hand-eye coordination and swing technique without fear of being hit by a pitched ball, and the defensive team is allowed more opportunities to develop fundamental fielding skills. Youngsters will learn to play and enjoy baseball and softball through good instruction and participation experience in Tee Ball.

A key to a successful Tee Ball program is the careful selection of managers and coaches. Adult leadership must reflect positive and constructive direction tempered with patience. Patience is probably the most important virtue necessary when managing youngsters of tee ball age. A pamphlet titled *Little League's Greatest Challenge* is available through Little League offices to assist league officials in selecting managers and coaches. *My Coach Says* and *The Other Side* are appropriate publications for the novice Tee Ball manager and are also available through Little League.

The learning experience must be fun coupled with developing fundamental skills of hitting, throwing, fielding and running. The basic concept should be total team participation in a congenial environment under the direction of concerned and competent adults. Remember, the value of the Tee Ball program is the learning experience. Participants in Tee Ball are in a critical developmental period. A manager's reward will come from being a positive factor and influence in each child's development.©

PONY Baseball/Softball

PONY is an international youth baseball and softball organization that provides thousands of young people with the opportunity to participate in these activities. PONY, the acronym for Protect Our Nation's Youth, is the second-largest youth baseball program in the world.

PONY Baseball was founded in 1951 in Washington, Pa., with only six local teams. Since its founding, the purpose of PONY has been to help young people develop into better adults through involvement in an organized sport.

Today there are approximately 29,000 registered PONY teams with about 400,000 young people participating in some area of the program. While the majority of the membership is located in the United States, there are teams in a number of other countries including Japan, Korea, Russia and Canada.

PONY offers baseball and softball in seven leagues for ages 5 through 18. The leagues are established on two-year age levels to insure developmental challenges and encourage player-to-player skills assistance while limiting the range of player ability within a program level.

The Shetland League, comprised of more than 2,500 teams for ages 5 and 6, is focused on instruction. All the players bat in order. Twelve players are used defensively, with four in the outfield and two extra infielders. Players are required to rotate so that they are exposed to the game at various positions. Two extra coaches may be used in the infield to give instruction under game conditions. A batting tee is used; there is no pitching.

The Pinto League (more than 4,000 teams) for ages 7 and 8 teaches basic game fundamentals and introduces the concept of competitive play. A batting tee is recommended, although adult pitchers or pitching machines may be used.

President Abraham Key tells T•BALL USA:

PONY Baseball strongly advocates the use of T-Ball as an introduction to baseball for young players. T-Ball should create an atmosphere of fun and instruction with an emphasis on player success.

Several of today's top professionals are PONY graduates. Ryne Sandberg, Brett Saberhagen, Andre Dawson and Cal Ripkin are just a few of the many major-league players who have participated in PONY programs.

PONY believes that teaching young people to play by the rules will help them learn to live by the rules. PONY stresses the development of self-esteem and the importance of being a team player. Youngsters who participate in PONY learn more than how to play the game. They also learn how to conduct themselves as quality individuals.

Babe Ruth League, Inc.

Founded in 1951 near Trenton, N.J., to provide wholesome amateur baseball for young teen-agers, the organization now has 855,000 participants, 43,000 teams, 6,200 leagues and 1.75 million volunteers. The Babe Ruth League had its first World Series in 1952, and that event is now held for each of its five age-range divisions.

T-Ball is played by nearly 5,000 teams in the Bambino Division, which began in 1952 for younger players, and a player must be 5 years old in order to participate. Babe Ruth League rules for T-Ball suggest having all players present batting in order, the inning over when all players have batted or when three outs have been made (whichever comes first), a hit ball must travel at least 25 feet and three strikes are an out. A regulation game is six innings; each player must play a minimum of two.

The Sportsmanship Code of Babe Ruth Baseball best describes its instructions to participants:

- Develop a strong, clean, healthy body, mind and soul.
- Develop a strong urge for sportsman-like conduct.
- Develop understanding of and respect for the RULES.
- Develop courage in defeat, tolerance and modesty in victory.
- Develop control over emotions and speech.
- Develop spirit of cooperation and team play.
- Develop into real, true CITIZENS.

©1954 Babe Ruth League, Inc.

Babe Ruth League graduates on recent major-league rosters include Cal Ripkin Jr., George Brett, Don Mattingly, Dave Justice, Mike Scioscia, Ryne Sandberg and at least 175 others. Carl Yastrzemski, Joe Morgan, Jim Palmer and Rod Carew are BRL graduates in the Baseball Hall of Fame. Both the presidents of the National and American leagues have recognized the accomplishments and success of the Babe Ruth League youth program.

Dixie Youth Baseball, Inc.

Founded in 1955, this organization provides a baseball program in 11 states in the
South and Southwest. A national board of
directors establishes policy and rules. The
national organization supports individual state
groups, each of which operates with unpaid,
volunteer officials. The program is designed as a recreational outlet
solely for the enjoyment of youngsters age 12 and under with an
emphasis on participation and sportsmanship and on developing the
basic playing skills of all players. Dixie Youth breaks down team
membership into the following divisions:

A Division "T-BALL" ....Players age 6 and under
AA Division ....Players age 8 and under
AAA Division ....Players age 10 and under
Majors Division ....Players age 12 and under

Each league has the authority to determine the age limits within
its own divisions during regular-season play.

The A and AA divisions (T-Ball and Coach-Pitch) are used as
a training program to teach fundamentals to younger, less experienced players. Each state organization adopts its own playing rules
for A and AA division play.

All matters relating to local league play are under the exclusive
supervision of a franchised league that operates within a defined
boundary. Any sanctioned tournament play is under the exclusive
supervision of a district director, who is a volunteer elected by the
leagues in each district.

Commissioner Wes Skelton writes:

Every franchised league is encouraged to provide a baseball program for its community that gives all the youth the opportunity to play the great national pastime while providing the best adult leadership possible. The role of managers and coaches is encouraged to include not only instruction in playing skills, but, by example, teaching the importance of hard work, self-discipline, dignity and good sportsmanship.

Each franchised league must meet all qualifications of Dixie Youth Baseball prior to receiving a certificate of franchise issued by the commissioner. Franchise fees are $6 per team; there are no fees assessed leagues for T-Ball teams.

Local league officials adopt their own rules in regard to the placement of players on team rosters. Leagues that wish to participate in tournament play submit team rosters to their district director.

Dixie Youth Baseball, Inc. fields between 1,200 and 1,300 leagues with about 8,500 to 9,000 T-Ball teams playing each season.

Dizzy Dean Baseball, Inc.

The organization is designed to allow as many youths as possible to participate in a fair and equal community baseball program regardless of sex, religion, race or color. If facilities are available, no youth shall be turned down. From a small beginning in 1962 as a part of Dixie Baseball (the name was changed to Dizzy Dean Baseball in 1975) there are now leagues in 19 states: Alabama, Arkansas, Colorado, Florida, Georgia, Illinois, Indiana, Kentucky, Louisiana, Maryland, Michigan, Mississippi, Missouri, New York, Ohio, Oklahoma, South Carolina, Tennessee and Texas. Leagues are established via franchise within communities or by smaller towns coming together to form a league with at least four teams. A state director is responsible for administration within each state but local officials may make certain decisions (such as player selection methods and number of games) about how the game is played in their community.

The game is played on a baseball field suitable to the physical development of growing youngsters. Managers, coaches and umpires are selected by community recreation leaders and league officers. They are educated, tested and certified by each state organization.

Commissioner Marion P. Pearson Sr. writes:

A lot of pressure is being placed on our youth today by parents and coaches who are trying to relive their own youth through their children. We must allow our young people to enjoy participation in our baseball program by teaching positive values. We must allow them to make their own mistakes. We must teach them how to accept responsibility for

*their actions and thus become better able to grow physi-
cally, mentally and emotionally. One negative parent (or
coach) can damage the self-esteem of any young person. I
am asking every league president to take control of "out-of-
control" parents or coaches....*

Dizzy Dean has several youth divisions. T-Ball has been spe-
cifically organized for ages 5 and 6; Farm League (with coach-
pitch and player-pitch) for ages 5-8. There are about 600 leagues
with approximately 60,000 players, mostly boys. The purpose of
the program is to provide a recreational outlet for as many youths
as possible, with emphasis being on local league play. However,
district and state tournaments are held for leagues wishing to participate.

Tee Ball® Baseball

This program was started in Florida in 1960 for children who were too young to play regular baseball. Since its inception, tee ball has been the foundation of the Gospel Projects Youth Athletic Club's community baseball program.

In 1987, the Pre-Tee Ball program was established to include young 4-year-olds and younger 5-year-olds. With a smaller playing field, fewer innings and rules that better fit these small youngsters, this program has become a success. Including little ones who would not normally play in organized sports at such an early age has proved to be a worthwhile endeavor.

In 1992, Pro-Tee was begun for 5-year-olds who were not able to play with their 6- and 7-year-old counterparts. Pro-Tee solved this problem by creating a league exclusively for this age level. A four-inning game using regular tee ball rules became a welcome addition to the overall program with benefits for parents as well as the players. By the following year, a significant difference in ability and interest was noticed among the (now) 6-year-olds who had played the previous year in Pro-Tee. The 6- and 7-year-old program was strengthened and 5-year-olds were participating in a league of their own.

The full program offers machine-pitch, girls' softball and regular fast-pitch baseball for youngsters up to 14 years old, but tee ball is the predominate sport that feeds all the other games and produces interested and excited ballplayers.

Commissioner Dayton Hobbs writes:

The thrust of our program is participation, not winning. Although we believe that competition is healthy for this age group and excellence (the prerequisite for winning) is to be strived for, having fun and enjoying the game is what our program is all about. Enjoyment of the game is what is important to the children. When the game ceases to be fun, it ceases to be a game. We urge parents, and insist that managers and coaches, not put pressure on children but attempt to teach them to play the game to the best of their ability while they enjoy it.

We ask adults to make every effort to set a proper example by their actions: to applaud all players or teams, never yelling against any player on any team, to show sportsmanship and to remember that **this is nothing more than a game of children's baseball.**

Youth Baseball Athletic League™

YBAL™ is a noncompetitive, co-ed, success-oriented, instructional T-Ball and baseball league. It is designed to teach players the basic fundamentals of baseball on an individual basis. Each child is given the opportunity to be successful at his or her own level of playing ability and maturity. Kids ages 4 to 14 play in a positive and safe environment where the focus is on fun and learning skills.

The league began in 1988 in Palo Alto, Calif., with four teams and 40 kids and now has more than 250 teams in Arizona, California, Iowa, Nebraska and Virginia. YBAL plans to expand into Colorado, Nevada, New Mexico, Florida and Hawaii by the end of 1996. Chuck Alley, founder/commissioner writes, "Our growth is due to our philosophy and dedication to offer a quality sports program that gives the game of baseball back to the kids."

Two of YBAL's four divisions use the batting tee. There are no outs, game scores or league standings in these early age groups. Every player takes the field and bats every inning. In the field, players are rotated in positions and the ball thrown "around the horn." There are three certified coaches on the field for each team.

- The Midget Division for 4- and 5-year-olds is T-Ball. This is an introduction to baseball and its basic skills. Players hit a practice ball and a "home run" ball. Games are two innings or 45 minutes and played on Saturday mornings. There are no practices during the week.

- The Junior Division is for 6- and 7-year-olds. This is an intermediate level of baseball with some advanced skill development. Each player hits a practice ball off the tee

73

and then at a coach-pitched ball. Games are three innings or one hour on Saturday mornings with no weekday practices. A skill building session is held before each game.

The Sandlot and Triple A divisions are for the older children. They offer traditional style baseball but with a few YBAL elements added; especially six station pregame clinics that focus on specific aspects of baseball.

"YBAL is baseball in its purest form," says Barry Wiess, superintendent of the Palo Alto Parks and Recreation Department and a former college coach. "The kids come off the field with smiles on their faces. They're having a great time and enjoying the game as they learn proper baseball technique."

Little League Baseball, Canada

The Canadian program operates under the same basic rules and philosophy as the U.S. game. The T-Ball program started in 1970 and currently fields 176 leagues with about 30,000 boys and girls participating. Coach-pitch is offered. Innings are determined by the bat-around rule or 3 outs. Scores are kept.

Marthe Dubroy, regional coordinator, advises that the T-Ball program is under the direct control of the parent board of directors. She adds, "Through careful selection and training of coaches and managers, the T-Ball program offers youngsters (ages 5 through 7) a venue whereby they can learn fundamental baseball skills and have fun at an early age."

Ancaster, Ontario

T-Ball play began in this small town near Hamilton in 1962 because, according to an official, "there were so many youngsters not old enough for Little League who were clamoring to play." The popularity of the game spread and in 1970 a tournament was held for out-of-town teams, which has evolved into a large-scale international invitational. On the its 25th anniversary, Jean Chrétien, the prime minister of Canada, stated to the participants that:

> *T-Ball offers you a wonderful opportunity to test your talent and skill against those of other teams, as well as establish friendships with players from around the world. Moreover, you will gain an understanding of the importance of good sportsmanship, fair play and teamwork.*

The Ancaster game is for 7- and 8-year-olds. Each team has 11 players with the two extra players in the outfield. Every player bats in each of the five innings in the game. The Ancaster committee is firm in its promotion of the values of family, fun and friendship and trusts that parents, coaches and managers will share them.

International Baseball Association

The International Baseball Association (IBA) is the international governing body for amateur baseball, officially recognized by the International Olympic Committee (IOC). The organization is responsible for sanctioning all official international, regional and world competitions for baseball at all age levels, establishing the eligibility requirements for baseball participants in international competitions. The IBA consists of 99 international member country federations and five continental confederations, including Europe, Asia, Africa, Oceania and the Americas. T-Ball is actively and extensively played in such diverse countries as Portugal, Zimbabwe and the Philippines.

National Sports Foundation

In 1965, the National Sporting Goods Association created The Sports Foundation to encourage participation in sports and recreation activities by recognizing the best and most innovative programs of the nation's park and recreation departments. The 1995 Gold Medal Awards were presented to departments in these five locales: Johnson County Park and Recreation, Shawnee Mission, Kan.; Tempe Community Services, Tempe, Ariz.; Schaumburg Park District, Schaumburg, Ill.; Columbus Parks and Recreation, Columbus, Ind.; and Naples Community Services, Naples, Fla.

Sports Foundation president Jack Schlicht said, "We are proud to recognize these winners because they represent the best programs among the hundreds of P&R departments across the country....the big winners are people who take advantage of these fun and beneficial programs."

T•BALL USA contacted each of the winning departments to learn how the game has been integrated into its activity and what elements have contributed to its success within the overall programs. The response from Jerry Judkins in Tempe, Ariz., is representative:

Stress the basic fundamentals of the game. Teach sportsmanship and life skills such as fairness, making friends and helping other people. Keep the rules simple and make sure everyone participates equally. Train staff and coaches to communicate with parents and children. Also, have patience with children. Create fun and interesting practices. Teach the kids about drugs and to be better people when they grow up.

The most-mentioned factors were the need for good staff (such as a program coordinator to oversee the operation and site supervisors to administer the games and work with parents) and the hiring of coaches trained to teach T-Ball.

Community League Organizers

T•BALL USA requested information from a cross section of leagues, large and small, in all parts of the country. From the responses received, the following are presented as they represent four very different programs: a YMCA, a parent-run group, a municipal department and an inner-city league.

Our program emphasizes the values of respect, responsibility, honest caring and faith through sport. We try to get as many children involved in the program as we can. Children are allowed to play with their friends and schoolmates. We have adopted an "athletes first, winning second" philosophy which is stressed to all coaches through the American Sport Education's Rookie Coaches course. There are no standings, tournaments, MVPs or All Star teams. Every player plays in the field and bats. There are no bench warmers. No scores are kept. Everybody is a winner at the Y.

We encourage parents to become actively involved at the practices and games. We feel it is important that parents utilize the time to participate in the development of children. We tell the parents up front that the program is not a baby-sitting service. Coaches are recruited by asking parents to volunteer on the registration form. We have parent meetings if more volunteers are needed. Coaches are encouraged to recruit their players' parents as assistant coaches and are given shirts, hats and manuals. The key is to get as many parents as you can while stressing the importance of having fun versus winning.

Brian Haines
Cypress Creek YMCA
Houston, Texas

Kids are recruited for our program through distribution of flyers to schools and newspapers. All kids report to a field or meeting hall. We attempt to place kids from the same neighborhood on the same team. We feel it is important to let friends play together. We ask the parents' advice concerning the placement of brothers or sisters on the same team. Some parents feel very strongly against this arrangement. Kids are not divided into any talent group; placement can be done alphabetically or based on where kids live. We search out volunteer managers and coaches or use young teenage boys. We attempt to play a parent in the field near their son or daughter to encourage hands-on coaching. The field sometimes becomes quite crowded. No adult is allowed to touch the ball at any time. The use of the adults is to give specific skills to individual players, but this usually occurs only in the first few games.

Paul Kramer
Greater Cincinnati Knothole Baseball Association

During my freshman year of college I began to umpire youth T-Ball for the local league in my community. I was assigned to the league championship game, which went back and forth. In the last inning the visiting team was kept from scoring and lost the game. As I was walking off the field, a young player asked me, "Did we win?" I said, "No, you lost by one run." The player then looked at me and said, "Well, I had fun anyway." This is a great example of what youth sports should be about. Most young athletes don't care about winning or losing. It is the competition and social interaction that are important at this age.

As a youth league administrator, I believe that if children are exposed to positive activities at a young age they can learn to develop a love for the game that will last a lifetime. We must learn to somehow keep the negative influence out of youth sports. This can be accomplished by education and the use of positive reinforcement.

Jeff Murray
Parks and Recreation Department
Oklahoma City, Okla.

We hang up signs on lamp posts near our recreation center. Managers are selected from a volunteer corps from specific wards in the city. Coaches are chosen from parents and must be certified through NYSCA programs. Things that have made our program work include:

(A) Parental involvement — I set up various drill stations which parents conduct based on instructional sheets I give them before the season. We also have picnics after every game.

(B) Hand-eye coordination — to help the players see the ball more effectively, I'll use balls with numbers painted on them. The kids have to identify the number as it comes to them.

(C) Relay drills — I'll have a group of players at second base and another at home plate. Each player takes a turn running the bases; the group that finishes first wins.

In the inner city, where there's an abundance of single-parent households, we have special problems and a heavy reliance on public transportation. Nevertheless, we are able to attend major- and minor-league games as special events for our teams.

Alfred Scott
The Senators T-Ball League
Washington, D.C.

Activity Survey

T•BALL USA surveyed a representative sample of league organizers: park and recreation departments, YMCAs, parent or community groups, and local units of national youth baseball leagues. The responses summarized below will provide information for both families and game staff.

Biggest problems with parents

- Try to push kids too hard, too fast; over-expectations.
- Scheduling conflicts with their lifestyle.
- Unfamiliar with game rules and league regulations.
- Pressure; stress on competition.
- Try to relive their childhood through their kids.
- Not prepared to volunteer; inconsiderate of volunteers' time.
- Drop off kids (sometimes late) and not stay to assist.
- Overzealous rooting.
- Forget that the game is a learning process for children.
- Lack of appreciation for coaches and league officials.
- Remembering that there are other children on a team.
- Talking to the coaches during the game.
- Don't have time to play/practice with kids at home.
- Over-involved or not involved.

Biggest problems with kids

- Short attention span; staying focused.
- Parents and grandparents.
- Unmotivated to practice and improve.

- Equipment not correct for size.
- Little attention to safety.
- Converging on a hit ball.
- Teasing; taunting.
- Lack of respect for authority.
- Little knowledge of baseball.
- Having so many other things to do.

Things that make programs work

- Emphasis on participation and fun.
- Fair and equal treatment for all players and coaches.
- Balanced teams.
- Solid volunteers and parental participation.
- An atmosphere of enjoyment and learning.
- Coaches and parents with great attitudes.
- Quality supervisors.
- Handle problems immediately.
- Good communications with parents and staff.
- Support from local business community.
- Equipment that lasts.
- NYSCA certified coach training.
- No win-loss records or stats kept.
- Certificates of participation for all players.
- Certificates of appreciation for coaches.
- Short season (8-10 games) for youngest players.
- Parent meeting before season starts.
- Let parents stand on field with first-year players.
- Experienced program administrator.
- Good playing field conditions.
- Priority on safety.
- Postgame beverages.

Ed Iacovo of the Stamford, Conn., Park and Recreation Department lists four elements that have made that city's program successful:

1) A noncompetitive, instructional league.

2) No scores are kept.

3) Everyone bats in the inning.

4) The 5- and 6-year-olds hit off the tee; 7- and 8-year-olds have the option to be pitched to by a coach, but after four pitches and no contact they bat from the tee.

These same components were often repeated in many of the responses received from leagues of various sizes and affiliations in all parts of the country.

Prospective families learn about program by:

- Printed handout
- Local paper
- Word of mouth
- Parents call in
- Mailing
- Bulletin board
- Local TV and radio
- Community calendar

Biggest needs

- Sponsor solicitation help
- Fund-raising plans
- Aids for local publicity
- New equipment
- Underwriting uniform costs
- Professional safety tips
- News about other leagues
- General info about the game
- Reading material on T-Ball for parents, kids and coaches

Popular special events

- End-of-season party
- Awards ceremony
- Parents vs. kids game
- Exhibition game

General team data

- Players per team — 10 to 20; average — 14
- 65 percent boys; 35 percent girls
- Cost per player — $15 or less, 25 percent; between $15 and $30, 55 percent; more than $30, 20 percent.

Equipment

T•BALL USA has consulted with league administrators, managers, coaches, sports safety experts and parents to determine the standards for equipment best suited for the participants in the game. The information received was evaluated and details may be found on pages 109-110 in the Recommended Rules of Play section of this book. A group of well-known and long-experienced manufacturers is now producing products to these specifications, which are identified with our logo as official T•BALL USA merchandise. Prices, where noted, are suggested retail.

Balls

Spalding

Two balls: one designed for game play and one for practice. Both are 9 inches in circumference and feature high-quality, white PVC covers with red stitching. The game ball has a soft polyurethane core and is recommended for all game and team practice situations. $3.50. The practice ball has a super-soft rubber core and is ideal for both team and individual practice sessions. $2.50.

Bats

Spalding

Two sizes: different length, weight and diameter. Each made of aircraft alloy aluminum with spun end and rubber grip. 26 inches long, 20 ounces, 2¼ inches diameter, or 25 inches long, 19 ounces, 2 inches diameter. Less than $ 22.00. Suitable for team play and practice.

Ball gloves

Spalding

Two styles based on age and size of player. Each is constructed of high-quality synthetic leather, easy-flex materials. Smaller 9-inch glove for players 5-7 years old has traditional open back design and single post-open web. $13.99. Larger 10-inch glove for ages 7 and older has open back design and pro catch closed web. $14.99. Both for use in games and practice.

Batting tees

Spalding

Game tee is a two-piece adjustable metal rod with heavy duty rubber tubing. Plate is an institutional grade white rubber base. 34-inch maximum height. $29.99. Practice tee with ball attached is two-piece plastic and rubber tubing, adjustable to 32 inches. Plate is white rubber base which has an anchor for the (removable) nylon cord and T-Ball. $17.99.

Athletic footwear

Comfort and fit are the critical elements in selecting the right shoes for sports
participation. Athletic footwear with
leather upper materials will provide dura-
bility, breathability and the kind of support that a child's foot needs. Shoes made
with rubber outer soles provide superior
cushioning and traction that is also impor-

Mercury International

tant for the youngster beginning in an active team game. Recognizing that children's feet grow quickly, price range is $13.00-$15.00.

Uniforms

Most leagues use T-shirts
with an organization or team
name screened on the front and
sponsor identification on the
back. The shirts with these basic graphics and any other
customization (player name and
number, etc.) are ordered through
local sporting goods dealer or
suppliers of team products.
Trimmed V-neck and pinstriped
jerseys are also popular. The official T•BALL USA uniforms illustrated here and elsewhere in
the book are made by the BIKE
Athletic Company in several
styles and in a broad range of
colors and come with the sleeve

Bike Athletic Company

patches. The 100 percent cotton T-shirt is approximately $11.95
and the 60/40 cotton/poly trimmed V-neck is approximately $19.95.
Double-knee pull-up pants are also available in the $9.95 range.

Headwear

DYOT   Outdoor Cap Company

Baseball caps are worn for function in the game and for fun off the field at home, to school or for playtime. Young T-Ball players can wear their sport with pride. The official team cap matches the BIKE uniform colors. Made by the Outdoor Cap Company, it has a foam front, padded visor and mesh back with plastic snap. $3.50. The recreational cap from DYOT is poly/cotton in white with red baseball-style stitching and red or blue visors. $10.00. Adult version has COACH embroidered on visor. $12.00.

Safety helmet

Although T-Ball play involves no pitching or (with older boys and girls) a ball coach-pitched in a friendly manner, organizers, coaches, parents and the children should not let this lull them into a feeling that helmets aren't important. The dangers from a batted ball as well as from a thrown ball are very real at this level.

ADAMS USA

The ADAMS USA batter's helmet is the only youth helmet made from polycarbonate alloy, a very tough space-age material. Sized for the youth player, it allows a full range of motion. The helmet is EVA foam-lined for comfort, comes equipped with snaps for chin strap attachment and is predrilled for a face guard. All ADAMS helmets meet NOCSAE standards for performance and are regularly tested by an independent laboratory to insure quality. $9.95-$12.95.

Safety protection

All athletic equipment is designed for a particular purpose. Much of it is protective, designed to make the game safer, which helps makes performance better. Doctors, coaches and sports trainers agree that use of an athletic supporter protects players from injury, fights fatigue, helps prevent strain, and provides support and comfort.

Size and quality are the most important considerations. The BIKE Athletic Company has been making athletic supporters since 1874 and has a range of specific safety products for T-Ball players of all ages.

The Little Line-up Card™

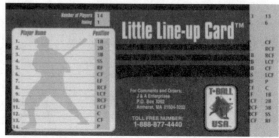

J&A Enterprises

An experienced T-Ball coach has invented a unique device to assist coaches in the placement of players in positions on the field. The LLC helps coaches make decisions easily and insures that players are distributed in a fair and orderly manner. It maximizes each player's opportunity of playing all positions equally during the season.

The LLC is made of card stock paper in two parts: an outer sleeve with viewing windows and a sliding insert for the players' names. The coach can reassign positions each inning by sliding the insert and matching players to their new positions.

What to Ask
at the Sporting Goods Store

What do you look for when buying your child's first equipment? Jim Steele, owner of The Sports Den in Fort Wayne, Ind., and long experienced in dealing with this question, provides the following advice:

You have signed your child up for a sport and now you must be certain he or she is equipped properly. For most parents, this means a trip to the toy department of the local department store, a quick glance at the equipment and selection based on very little information. While this isn't the worst thing a parent can do, there are some definite decisions that should be considered before making any purchases. Based on 17 years of coaching experience, 20 years of owning a sporting goods store, and raising and coaching five sons and daughters through many years of organized sports, not to mention living on ballpark hot dogs and colas, I would like to make the following suggestions for all parents.

1) Before buying any equipment, check with the league or coach to find out what equipment the league will provide and what equipment you will need to purchase. For example, many baseball leagues provide balls and bats but each individual player needs to provide his own glove.

2) When making the purchase it is not necessary to buy the best, most expensive item on the market until you are certain that your child is going to stick with the sport and enjoy it. For instance, when your child starts to play T-Ball it is not wise to spend $80 on the first pair of athletic

shoes until he is sure it is a sport he wants to pursue seriously.

3) Find a sporting goods store with employees who have knowledge of what they are selling. The employee should know more about the equipment than you do.

4) Always be certain the equipment meets safety standards. The most important thing about your child's participation in a sport is his safety. For instance, baseball helmets should be N.O.S.A.C. safety approved.

5) Check local and national league rule books to make certain that the equipment meets the standards of the organization that your child will be participating in. A reputable sporting goods store will have employees who will know this information or be able to tell you where to find it.

Basic Skills

Coaches' Instructions for Families

It is the responsibility of the coaches to instruct and drill their players in the skills required to play the game. There are books and videos devoted to this subject, but these are usually focused on baseball as played by older children.

T-Ball parents and other family members and friends need to be aware of the most basic fundamentals so that they can:

■ Work at home with the player on individual skill practice in an off-the-playing field activity.

■ Answer questions and remind the child of what has been taught by the coaches.

■ Understand what has to be accomplished in terms of physical action and personal performance.

■ Make practice fun in a noncompetitive setting while helping the youngster improve the required skills.

■ Better judge for themselves the progress being made by the player in actual league game play.

T•BALL USA has gathered the advice of experienced coaches from programs in all parts of the country. Based on this information, the following checklist provides a step-by-step guide for families when working with their youngsters to improve basic skills.

■ **Batting — the stance, swing and follow-through.**

• Adjust the tee with ball set even to the hitter's waist.

• Face tee with feet spread shoulder-width apart.

- Bend knees, body in slight crouch.
- Weight on balls of feet.
- Grip bat, hands together above the knob.(Photo 1)
- Hold bat firmly; don't squeeze.
- Bring bat up and away from the body. (Photo 2)

Photo 1

Photo 2

- Keep shoulders level; bat and head steady.
- *Eyes on the ball.*
- Short step with the front foot at start of swing.
- *Swing level* and bring the bat through the center of the ball. (Photo 3)
- Watch bat hit ball; keep head down.
- Weight shifts to front foot; back foot stays on the ground.

Photo 3

Photo 4

- Extend arms and follow through; swing around. (Photo 4)
- Drop the bat; *do not throw it.*

■ **Catching — remember:**

- *Eyes on the ball.*
- *Watch the ball go into the glove.*
- *Cover the ball with the other hand.*

Ground ball

- Stand legs apart, shoulder-width or wider.
- Bend knees. Get low. Lean forward. (Photo 5)
- *Run to the ball.*
- Keep body in front of ball.
- Glove low to the ground.
- Scoop or catch the ball and cover it. (Photo 6)

Photo 5

Photo 6

Fly Ball

- Run to where the ball is going.

- Call for the ball: "I've got it."

- Stop and wait for the ball.

- Hands together, fingers up, shoulder high or over the head.

- Watch ball into glove and cover.

Thrown ball

- Bend knees slightly.

- Watch the ball.

On a ball thrown to player above the waist

- Hands together facing out; thumbs up.

- Catch and cover.

On a ball thrown below the waist

- Hands together; little fingers touching. (Photo 7)

- Catch and cover.

Photo 7

Photo 8

■ **Throwing — grip and motion.**

- Thumb under the ball.

- Two or three fingers on top.

- Don't worry about the seams.

- Eyes on the target.

- Legs apart; foot on throwing arm side behind the body.

- Arm back and up, front shoulder turned toward target.

- *Step toward target with foot opposite the throwing arm.*
  Right-hander with left foot; left-hander with right foot.
  (Photo 8)

- Push off on back foot as throw begins; end with weight
  on forward foot.

- Release the ball in front of the body and follow through.

■ **Baserunning:**

- Run on the balls of the feet.

- Pump arms back and forth.

- Watch and listen to the base coach for instructions such as hands up for "stop", windmill arm for "keep going."

After the ball is hit:

- Run behind the tee, unless left-handed. (Photo 9)
- Look at first base, not where the ball has gone.
- Run outside the foul line; inside belongs to the fielder.
- Run straight through and past first base; don't jump

Photo 9

  on it or slow down. (First base coach to tell runner to turn toward or go to second base depending on where ball is hit and how played by the defense.)

When on base:

- Keep one foot touching the base until next batter hits the ball.
- Lean forward; when ball is hit, push off the base.
- Know where the ball is.
- When passing a base, try to touch it on the side without breaking stride.

Sliding (not recommended for the youngest players)

- Begin about four to five feet from the base.
- Arms up, fingers bent, chin down.
- Bend one leg under the other; looks like the figure 4.
- Lower leg hits ground, then the butt and back.
- Top leg (the extended one) touches the base.
- No head-first sliding.

Remember — repetition is the key to progress.

Skills Checklist for Parents

The Johnson County, Nebraska, Parks and Recreation District, organizers of one of the country's best-run T-Ball programs, tells parents to emphasize the following skill points:

Batting

- A level, even, downward swing is more likely to gain a hit.

- An uppercut swing is more likely to produce a pop-up or a foul ball.

- The batter should learn to look for the holes in the defense and hit through them.

- The batter should learn that the position of his or her feet will determine the flight of the ball.

- The batter should use a bat that is light enough to handle. The velocity of the swing, rather than the weight of the bat produces the long ball.

- Beginning batters must be taught to lay the bat down after hitting the ball.

- Batters should be taught the proper grip and stance.

Throwing

This is probably the weakest of all skill areas and one of the most difficult to remedy.

- Use the correct grip on the ball.

- Throw overhand.

- Use the whole body and follow through.

Baserunning

- Run immediately toward first base after hitting the ball.

- Do not run immediately from the base on a fly ball. Tag up.

- Don't watch the ball all the time, but learn to follow the instructions of the base coach.

- Run the bases with the emphasis on hitting the inside corners of the base.

- Run as fast as possible to and beyond first base. Don't slow down until the base is touched.

Fielding

- Position the body in front of the ball.

- Field the ball with both hands.

- Use the pocket of the glove, not the web.

- Throw the ball to the proper place as soon as possible after catching it. Do not just hold the ball.

- Back up all throws to the base.

Hitting Tips for T-Ball

Mike Jetel

Hitting is the most difficult task of all things in sports. For a T-Ball player it can be monumental. Therefore, patience and encouragement are critical elements when working with hitters.

Setting expectations that are too high can be frustrating to both parents and kids. Every child wants to do his or her best at anything he or she does. Telling the child to hit a home run may be out of reach for most players at this age. Encouraging the child just to hit the ball will probably go farther in bringing about the desired objective.

Place improvement and development ahead of winning at this point. With improvement and the development of skills, winning will come.

Make it fun! Make hitting practice fun! Everyone will enjoy the game more. Here are some important things to remember when working with young hitters:

- Choose a bat that is the right size for the hitter. It should be about the distance from the ground to the batter's waist. It should also be the lightest bat for its length.

- Make sure the hitter has a batting helmet that is the right size and meets all safety standards. If the helmet is too big it can slip down over the hitter's eyes. It will also protect the hitter from errant throws when he or she becomes a runner.

- Position the batting tee so the ball is at or near the hitter's waist. Also, it is very important that the tee is positioned in front of the regular home plate so the hitter learns to hit the ball out in front of home plate. Another way to do this if the base of the tee is the same shape as home plate is to position the tee with the apex or point of the base of the tee facing the pitcher's mound instead of aligning it to cover the shape of the regular plate.

■ When the hitter gets into the batter's box, make sure he or she is at a distance where the bat will strike the ball about three to four inches from the free end of the bat.

■ The hitter should assume a good athletic position. That is, spread the feet about shoulder-width. A slight crouch is also helpful. The feet should be positioned so that they are parallel with each other and pointing toward home plate. The forward most foot should be positioned where the plate angles toward the point. If the front foot is kept in this "closed" position, that is, pointed toward the tee during the complete swing, it will help to keep the hitter from "pulling his or her head off the ball" or away from the ball.

■ To properly position the bat to get ready to hit, start by gripping the bat with both hands. Make sure a right-handed batter has the right hand as the upper hand and a left-handed batter has the left hand in the upper position. Position the bat in the fingers of the hitter as much as possible making sure that the *knocking knuckles* are lined up. The knocking knuckles are the knuckles that you would use to knock on a door. They should be all in a row. There are a couple of ways to do this. If you can point the index fingers in the same direction at the same time they are probably in the correct position and the bat is being held correctly. Currently, a batting glove is being marketed that helps batters of all ages line up the hands and bat in the correct manner. It is called the Upper Hand. This will allow the hitter to have the fastest swing and most power.

- Start with the hands and bat in front of the chest and move them back about four to six inches to the "ready" position. The batter should take a couple of measuring strokes at the ball being careful not to actually hit the ball but just to measure the swing. The hitter should concentrate on looking at the ball the whole time as the swing comes forward. The swing should be a direct line to hit the ball. One thing that will help to avoid the uppercut swing is to keep the shoulders parallel to the ground or the front shoulder slightly lower than the back shoulder.

- Once the ball has been hit, the batter should run behind the tee to get to first base. Try to encourage the hitter to look at first base as he or she runs and not the ball after it has been hit.

- Do not try to teach all of these things at one session. Choose those things that the child is ready for. Work on each of these gradually or as the child progresses.

Remember — have fun.

Photo courtesy of BIKE Athletic Company

Recommended Rules of Play

T-Ball is offered within the programs of many national and regional organizations (primarily the youth baseball leagues), local YMCAs, park and recreation departments, and a variety of community and parent-run games. Local groups often develop playing rules based on their own specific needs and experience over the years.

T•BALL USA, via a survey and direct contact with league administrators from all types of organizations, large and small, in all parts of the country, has determined a suggested set of rules. These standards bring together the advice and recommendations of men and women with a direct knowledge of what has worked in successful programs where they have had active participation and responsibility.

Information about coach-pitch (where an adult throws the ball to the batter) and pre-tee ball (for the youngest players) will be found following this section.

Standardization of the regulations of the game so that it can be played in an identical manner everywhere by all types of youth-oriented organizations is a long-term goal of T•BALL USA.

Object of the Game

Members of two teams take turns hitting a ball off a batting tee set on home plate. Batters try to get on base and advance to home; fielders try to prevent that from happening. Scores are not kept and there are no winners or losers.

Playing Field

- The field of play is shared by an infield and an outfield, and is separated into fair and foul territory.

- The field is similar to dimensions of a youth baseball league-type field but with only 50 feet between the bases.

- The diamond is a square with a base at each corner.

- The bases include first, second and third base. They are made of canvas, soft, 15 inches square and about 2½ inches thick, and fastened in place.

- The playing line is an imaginary line running between first base and third base. It can also be an arc, a curved circle extending out 40 feet from the point of home plate.

- Home plate is made of white rubber, is five-sided and is set flush with the ground. It is 17 inches wide across the edge facing the infield, 8½ inches long on each side and 12 inches long on the sides of the point facing the catcher.

FIELD OF PLAY

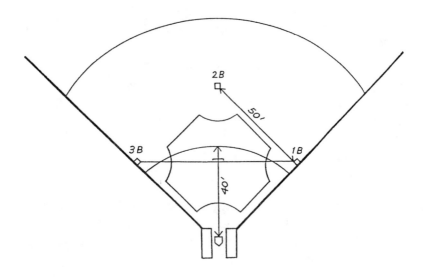

- The center of the pitcher's area is 38 feet from the point of home plate.

- The batter's boxes are to be 5 feet long by 3 feet wide. The batting tee is placed on home plate, 2 feet from the front edge of the boxes and 3 feet from their rear border.

- The outfield is the wide area of the playing field beyond the diamond and most distant from home plate.

- If there are outfield fences, they shall be 115 to 125 feet from the batting tee, with the maximum distance used by the 7- and 8-year-old players.

- The foul lines extend from home plate past first and third bases. Fair territory is the playing field within and including the foul lines; foul territory is the area outside the foul lines.

- A foul strike area is within an imaginary or drawn arc between the baselines, 10 feet out from the batting tee.

Official Equipment

- The bat is a smooth, rounded stick of wood (not laminated) or hollow metal (aluminum or other alloys). Length: 25 to 26 inches. Diameter: 2¼ inches, maximum. Weight: 17 to 20 ounces. Handles may have rubber grips or be taped. Color bats are permitted.

- The T-Ball shall measure between 9 and 9¼ inches around and weigh between 4 and 5 ounces. Softer than a standard baseball, it may have a molded vinyl core or a sponge rubber center and a hand stitched leather or synthetic cover.

- The batting tee is a moveable platform set on home plate with an adjustable, flexible tube to support the ball.

- A fielder's glove shall not be more than 12 inches long. The first base player may use a glove or a mitt (no fingers, except for the thumb), up to 12 inches. The catcher may wear a mitt of any size. Gloves may be of any weight.

■ Safety helmets must be made of high impact plastic and fully protect the head all around, the temples and ears. Helmets must not come off during hitting or baserunning.

Uniforms

■ Players dress in active sports apparel.

■ Athletic footwear with flat soles or soft, molded cleats is recommended.

■ Team T-shirts or baseball-style jerseys and caps are preferred, but not mandatory.

■ Team or league names are usually screened on the front of the shirts; local sponsor identification is best placed on the rear. Player numbers are optional.

■ Batters, on-deck batter, base runners and coaches must wear safety helmets.

■ The catcher must wear protective gear: mask, helmet, throat and shin guards, and chest protector with collar.

■ Boys are to wear athletic supporters; a protective cup is recommended.

■ No jewelry, watches or metal objects are allowed to be worn.

Teams and Leagues

■ A T-Ball roster (list of players on team) shall not include more than 20 boys and girls; 15 is preferred. Minimum for a game is 12 players. The roster may be changed anytime.

■ Players must be at least 5 years old and not turn 9 before August 1st in the calendar year in order to play.

■ Note: An introductory game exclusively for younger children to learn to play may be set with 30 feet between the bases, a 25-foot playing line and the foul ball zone arc at 5 feet from the batting tee. (See section on pre-tee ball.)

- Teams should try to have an equal number of players of the same age.

- A tryout system is recommended to rate and distribute the players among the teams.

- If all ages are playing together, as may happen in smaller communities, the older players are to be divided among the teams before the younger players.

- Players are to be assigned to their teams by a group decision by those adults (youth group staff, managers, coaches) concerned with the local organization and functioning of the game.

- Local groups may establish leagues, which are to be administered by community organizations (such as parks and recreation departments, school systems, YMCAs, municipal athletic programs, youth-oriented associations and sponsors, parent and volunteer groups)

- Where possible, each league should have six teams, with a maximum of 120 players. A 90-player limit per league is preferred, based on 15 players on a team.

- League teams are to play no less than 10 or more than 20 games in a season.

General Rules

- The game follows the basic regulations of baseball/softball, but is unique in that:
  - There is no pitching; the ball is hit off the batting tee.
  - There are no strikeouts.
  - As there is no pitching, there are no balls; therefore, no bases on balls.
  - Bunting and half swings are not allowed.
  - No stealing. Base runners cannot leave the base until the ball is hit.
  - All players on the team bat in each inning of play.

- When a team bats through the batting order once, the inning is over (the bat-around rule.)

- Suggested game length is four innings or a 90-minute time limit. The recommendation for younger players is 3 innings or one hour. No game should exceed six innings for any reason.

- Unlimited substitutions are permitted, but no player can be taken out of the game unless that player has batted one time and played one inning in the field.

- Defensive players are to alternate between the infield and the outfield every inning.

■ Standings are not kept; there are no championship games or awards, except for each player's participation.

■ Only players, managers, coaches and umpires are allowed on the playing field before and during a game. Coaches may be on the field to instruct defensive players, but cannot touch a ball in play. Coaches for the offensive team may give batting instructions, but cannot physically help runners on base.

■ When a team is at bat, all players are to sit on their bench in the order in which they will bat, except for the batter, the on-deck batter and any base runners. When a team is in the field, all substitute players must stay on their team's bench.

■ Managers and coaches may stand near players but not interfere with the game. They can ask the umpire for "time" to show or explain to a player what is to be done. Managers and coaches may also act as umpires, if needed.

■ No one (including spectators, coaches, managers and players) may argue with the umpire about a rule or a call involving judgment, but the coaches and managers may point out the existence or nonexistence of a rule to the umpire before the next play begins.

■ The umpire in his or her discretion may issue a warning to a team for unsportsmanlike conduct, such as taunting. A second infraction will cause a base on balls to be awarded to the batter or the first player up when the defensive team comes to bat.

Procedure

■ The starting lineup of each team shall include all the players.

■ The catcher stands far enough behind home plate so as to not interfere with the batter.

■ The player stationed in the pitcher's area acts as an infielder and stays in place until the ball is hit.

■ All the other infielders play in their positions and shall not cross the playing line until the ball is hit. If a player crosses the line, the umpire calls "time" and the ball is dead.

■ The infield positions have a player at each base and a shortstop between second and third bases. Additional players may be used to fill in the infield.

■ The outfield may consist of left, left-center, center, right-center and right fielders.

■ The game is divided into innings in which each team has a turn at bat (to hit the ball) and to be in the field.

■ When the defensive team is in place and ready, its manager tells the umpire, who then puts the ball on the tee and calls, "play ball."

Batting

■ The batter is not to touch the tee (coach or umpire may adjust the tee to the player's height.)

■ A fair ball is a batted ball that:
  • Lands in or is touched by a player in fair territory (infield or outfield).

- Bounces past first or third base on or over fair territory.

- First lands in foul territory, then rolls fair into the infield.

- Bounces on a base or touches a player or an umpire while in fair territory.

■ A foul ball is a batted ball that:

- Lands in or is touched by a player in foul territory.

- Touches a player or umpire in foul territory.

- Rolls into foul territory before reaching first or third base before being touched and comes to rest there.

■ A foul ball is called if the ball is hit into fair territory but travels less than 10 feet, or if the batter hits the tee and knocks the ball off.

■ If the batter throws the bat in a dangerous manner, the batter is out and any base runners must return to their base.

■ The batter becomes a runner when the ball is hit hard enough into fair territory in one of the following ways:

- In the air — if the ball is caught by a fielder before it touches the ground, the batter is out.

- On the ground — if a fielder can pick up the ball and get it to a teammate at first base (or make the play alone) before the batter arrives, the batter is out.

■ If a ball cannot be caught before it touches the ground and cannot be received at first base before the batter arrives, the batter has a single base hit and may stay safely at first base or try to run to other bases.

■ If the defensive team can get the ball to second or third base and tag the batter (touch with the ball or with the ball in the glove) before the batter arrives at a base or between the bases, the batter is out.

■ A hit that allows the batter to safely reach second base is a double; if the batter reaches third base, it is a triple.

■ On a home run, the batter runs around all the bases and crosses home plate, as do any teammates on base.

■ The infield fly rule (a fly ball hit above the infield with runners on first and second base or on first, second and third) does not apply. If caught, the batter is out; the ball is not in play and runners cannot advance.

Baserunning

■ The batter becomes a base runner, with the ball in play, if:

  • The ball is hit into fair territory.

  • A fielder makes an error (mishandles the ball.)

■ The batter goes to first base and the ball is dead if:

  • Fielder interference is called.

  • A fair ball strikes a base runner or umpire before the ball passes or touches a fielder.

■ A runner has a right to be at each base by getting there before being put out and can stay until legally advancing to another base or being forced to leave by the batter or another base runner.

■ A runner must remain on base until the ball is hit; if off the base when ball is hit, runner is out.

■ Two runners cannot be on the same base at the same time. The first to legally arrive is safe; the other runner may be tagged out. If the first runner is forced to advance and two runners are on base, the second runner has the right to the base.

■ When the ball is in play, a base runner may advance if:

  • A ball is hit into fair territory or thrown into fair or foul territory.

- After any fly ball is caught, but the runner must first tag up (touch the current base.)

- A fair ball hits a base runner or umpire after passing a fielder or touches a fielder.

■ A runner must return to the base after:
  - A ball is caught on the fly.
  - A foul ball is not caught.
  - Batter, runner or umpire interference.

■ A base runner is called out if the runner:

  - Is forced (made to advance) to another base and the fielder with the ball tags the runner or touches the base before the runner arrives.

  - Is tagged by a fielder and is not safely standing on base when the ball is in play.

  - Runs past first base safely, turns toward second and is tagged.

  - Runs more than three feet outside of a direct line between the bases to avoid being tagged.

  - Interferes with a player fielding a batted ball or with a thrown ball.

  - Is involved in a double play (two offensive players put out in the same action.)

  - Is hit by a fair ball while off base and before it passes any infielder.

  - Passes another runner or arrives last while another runner is on a base.

  - Leaves a base before a fly ball is caught and is tagged before returning.

  - Misses touching a base and a defensive player tags the runner or base.

  - Purposely kicks the ball or runs the bases backwards.

- The runner is not out if the runner:
  - Runs outside the base path to avoid interfering with a fielding attempt.
  - Touches and runs past first base but returns directly to it (must run past the base into foul territory.)
  - Is hit with a batted ball while standing on base.
  - Stays on base until a fly ball is touched, then tries to advance (can be tagged out at the next base.)
- If a fielder overthrows the ball, the runner is allowed one extra base.
- After players have moved ahead on the bases as far as possible or after an out, the umpire calls "time" and puts the ball back on the tee.

Summary of Recommended Rules

- Players' ages are 5, 6, 7 and 8.

- Players per team: 12 minimum, 20 maximum.

- 50 feet between the bases.

- Playing line between first base and third base or an arc 40 feet from home plate.

- Every player bats and plays in the field.

- Ball is hit off a batting tee; no pitching.

- There are no walks.

- No strikeouts.

- No stealing.

- Ball must travel 10 feet or is a foul.

- No fielder may cross the playing line until the ball is hit.

- An inning is over when all players have batted once.

- Standard game is four innings.

- Scores are not kept; no winners or losers.

- Safety helmets must be worn.

Coach-Pitch

One of the fastest growing aspects of T-Ball is coach-pitch, where an adult (or mature teen-ager) throws the ball to the player at bat. All of the regular T-Ball rules apply, except that no tee is used. An offensive coach pitches to his or her own batters. The defensive player in the pitcher position stands slightly behind and to the side of the coach-pitcher.

This variation of the game is usually reserved for teams of older players (6 years and up) or for younger players whose batting skills have advanced. In most situations, the coach delivers an agreed number of pitches; usually, five to seven. If the player is unable to hit the pitched ball, it is then placed on the tee and the batter's turn continues.

The West Branch YMCA in Omaha, Neb., has an outstanding program based on this alternative method of starting children in the sport of baseball. Tom Stubby, the program director, describes the essence of the game:

> The pitching is done by the coaches; each coach pitches to his own team. This enables the players to see the same person pitching to them during practices and games. Having the coach on the field helps some players to relax because they see their coach out there in front of them. It also helps the coach, because he knows where some players like the ball to help them get more hits to build their confidence. Coaches may also help the players with pointers while they are batting. Coaches use many different methods of delivering the ball to the plate. Some use the underhand pitch with a little arc to keep the speed down. Some coaches use the overhand pitch to the players, which gives them the option of the slow

arc or a slightly faster pitch. Most coaches who use the over-hand methods throw from one knee to put them on the same level as the players, making it easier for the players to see the ball. The overhand pitch also gets the players used to seeing the ball from the angle which they will see for the rest of their baseball careers. As coaches practice with their teams, they develop the method which allows them to throw strikes to their players. I have seen very few coaches stick to one method. Most coaches will use both depending on the ability of the individual player. If the player does strike out, the ball goes on the tee. By first using a pitched ball and then the tee, if necessary, the player can always be successful at the plate.

Starting off with coach-pitch helps the players develop the hand-eye coordination that is needed to track the ball. It also gives the players more of a feeling of playing like big-leagu-ers because they hit a ball that was thrown to them. The pitched ball also provides a little more activity and excite-ment to the game at this young age. Parents and spectators get the enjoyment of seeing the coach make the occasional bad pitch behind the hitter. Parents also get to see the extent of the progress of the players who couldn't hit very well early in the season and had to hit off the tee, to the players who start hitting the pitched ball for the first time. The whole concept of the coach-pitch method provides the quickest, saf-est way for the young players to learn the fundamentals needed to hit the ball in a supportive, caring environment.

T•BALL USA recognizes the benefits provided by coach-pitch and endorses its use; especially after the youngest of players have gained confidence in the batting situation.

Pre-Tee Ball

This program provides an introductory training and playing experience for youngsters not fully ready for regular T-Ball. Rule modifications:

Playing Field

- 30 feet between the bases.
- Outfield — 60 to 75 feet from the batting tee.
- Pitcher's area center — 25 feet from the tee.
- Imaginary playing line between first and third base or an arc 24 feet from home plate.
- Foul ball zone — 5-foot radius from the tee.

Teams

- Minimum for a game is eight on a side.
- Players to be 4 years old or 5-year-olds too young to play standard T-Ball. Mature 3½- year-olds may also be considered.
- A player who becomes too strong for pre-tee ball (advanced skills, safety risk to others, etc.) should be moved up into regular T-Ball.

General Rules

- Each player gets five swings at bat.
- Game length — 3 innings, maximum. One-hour time limit recommended. Innings must be completed.
- Bat-around rule applies.
- Offensive team may have coaches at all the bases and a hitting coach near the tee.
- Defensive team may have three coaches on the field.

■ Some rules may be relaxed if umpire or league organizers believe players are unable to fully participate in the game.

The Youth Athletic Club in Milton, Fla., has developed an effective pre-tee ball activity as an introduction for future play in its regular Tee Ball Baseball program. Based on their experience, club officials believe that the key to a successful and enjoyable season is to "teach each child two or three aspects of baseball and to do these well. Chaos breeds lack of interest." Their suggestions for coaches include:

1) As early as possible, assign each player a single position and teach the child to do **one** thing.

   A. Teach the pitcher and first baseman to get the ball, run to first, and touch the base.

   B. Teach fielders to catch the ball and tag a runner, if possible, holding on to the ball with both hands.

   C. Teach outfielders to pick up the ball, run to second or third base and tag a runner, if possible.

NOTE: This age player will almost never know when to tag the runner or the base. Yelling at the player during a play will only confuse the child. Therefore, teach the pitcher and the first baseman to touch the bag and all other players to touch the runner.

2) Insist that each child play their position and not run after every ball.

3) Teach each child to swing the bat, set the bat down and run to first base.

4) As a player is running to a base, or is at a base, he or she should be taught to look at the base coach and do what the coach says.

T•BALL USA recognizes that many 4-year-olds have the physical ability and emotional stability to begin to play in an organized team game, but careful and impartial parental participation is required. The emphasis must be focused on the fun involved in the sport experience and the learning of certain skills; not on winning.

Pitching Machine

A significant number of leagues are now using pitching machines with the older (7 and 8 year) age groups and/or as a training device for more advanced younger players. It is a stage beyond coach-pitch and, under proper control and supervision, can be considered as an option for qualified players.

Tom Barnes, director of Parks/Recreation/Forestry in Whitewater, Wis., and responsible for youth sport activity, has had extensive experience with the pitching machine and passes on these comments:

- Increase defensive opportunity; promote batting confidence; develop the entire team; play the game in less time....sound too good to be true? Then you haven't tried implementing a youth baseball program that uses a pitching machine instead of a coach.

- Using a machine that can deliver strikes at a predetermined speed will benefit the greatest number of children. Players will gain confidence in their ability to "put the bat on the ball," make them more aggressive at the plate and encourage more baserunning. There is no concern that the adult pitcher may be overpowering, intimidating or wild.

- Defensively, the ball will be put in play more often, resulting in a greater number of defensive chances. Ironically, more players will be willing to play catcher, as they know each pitch will always be in the strike zone.

As an administrator, coach and parent, I am very pleased with the use of the pitching machine. The concept is excellent for a recreation program and good training for players interested in pursuing higher levels of competition.

For Kids

T-Ball is a baseball game for young boys and girls. It is a way to have fun while learning how to play. There are no winners or losers.

Here are some important things to know:

- The ball is not pitched. It is hit off a batting tee.
- Every player bats and plays in the field.
- There are no strikeouts or walks (bases on balls).
- There is a real or pretend playing line between first and third bases or curved 40 feet out from home plate.
- No fielder can cross the playing line until the ball is hit.
- The ball must be hit at least 10 feet or it is a foul.
- When the ball is hit, don't throw the bat.
- Runners must stay on base until the ball is hit. There is no stealing.
- The inning is over when all players have batted one time.
- Safety helmets must be worn when at bat or on base.

Listen to the coaches. Your league may have some different rules, like keeping score or having a coach pitch to the batter. That's part of the game, too.

Remember — have fun and be a good team player.

T-Bears

The official T•BALL USA mascots are crafted in black or brown surface washable plush fabric and wear logoed T-shirts. 6 inches approximately $7.50 retail; 10 inches approximately $12.95. From Market Identity.

Successful Fund Raising

An important factor in the long-term success of any T-Ball organization is the ability to finance the administration of the season, the acquisition of equipment and the maintenance of facilities. For most leagues this translates into the need to raise funds on a consistent basis. While this may seem like a difficult task, when the correct products are used to achieve the funding goal, the solicitation process can proceed effectively. League administrators and parents who become involved in the financial support of their children's teams need to understand how the right approach can enhance profitability, with benefits on several levels.

T•BALL USA asked one of the country's leading fund-raising companies, World's Finest Chocolates, Inc. of Chicago, to describe the key components in a successful program. The company advises:

The primary goal of any fund-raiser is clear — the league needs to earn money for the present and the future. This is achieved by offering for sale a product that generates a high profit to the organization. Once you have decided what type of item is appropriate, the next step is to select one that will be easy to sell within your community. The most important thing to keep in mind is quality, which not only sells the product for the current season but also lays the groundwork for years to come.

A good example of this is the World's Finest Milk Chocolate and Almond Bar. In addition to good taste and good value, the label of the bar has three characteristics that are key contributors to the success of the fund-raiser.

■ *Personalization*: The bars can be customized with the name of your organization, league or team printed on the wrapper. This unique service legitimizes the sale to the customer. There is no question in his mind where the money is going when the label boldly states your group's name plus a "thanks for your support" message.

■ *Recognition*: The white wrapper with the silver foil lining is well known across the country for the high quality chocolate inside. The product will sell itself, and does so year after year.

■ *Coupons*: Each bar has a valuable coupon from national fast-food chains on the reverse of the wrapper. They range from $1 to $2 when redeemed. The ability to offer a product to a customer that is of the best quality and also pays for itself the next time the buyer goes to a participating restaurant is something to be looked for when choosing a fund-raiser.

Profitability: The bars are ideal for fund raising. There are $1 and $2 versions with a profit margin of at least 50 percent. For every dollar sold, half will go directly to the league.

Customer Service: Another key element to consider is the flexibility that the fund raiser can offer as the sale progresses. This becomes important if the sale is running better than initially expected or is, perhaps, going slower. In these situations, a national company like World's Finest can adapt to make your sale the most profitable. If you are going to run out of product, we can deliver more in a matter of days from our regional warehouses. In the event you have unsold product, we will accept returns of full cases, opened or unopened, at the end of your sale. Also, we have a network of distributors to provide you with a local representative to answer questions and give helpful hints to enhance your program. Flexibility and service should be sought when selecting a fund-raising company for your league.

Incentives: An important part of the activity is to make it fun and interesting for the people doing the selling. Perhaps the most effective way is to use prizes as incentives. They not only add excitement and enthusiasm to the project, but help set and accomplish specific goals. Prizes can vary greatly. They can be trips to popular places, stuffed animals, electronics or a range of local options. Whatever they may be, it is important to use a fund-raising company that can accommodate your needs. To fund these essential incentives, we have developed a proven system to generate prizes for children, parents and other family members, coaches and volunteers.

Economic realities have made fund raising a necessity. If the correct choices are made prior to the T-Ball season, this part of your needs can be transformed into a positive and rewarding activity. For more information about World's Finest Chocolate, see the Reference section of this book.

Licensed Products

The T•BALL USA™ name and logo will be licensed to qualified manufacturers of appropriate products for national distribution to retailers, primarily in the popular price range. Official merchandise includes:

SPALDING®   Sports Equipment

MERCURY   Athletic Footwear

BIKE®   Uniforms and Active
          Sports Products

ADAMS
USA   Safety Helmets

OUTDOOR CAP   Team Uniform Caps

 Patches and Emblems

 Drinkware

 Mascot Animals
and Figures

 Fund Raising

J&A Enterprises Lineup Cards

Revenue from the sales of licensed products will be used to further the stated goals and programs of the T•BALL USA Association.

SPALDING ®

Offical Product of T●BALL USA

Game Tees

Practice Tees

Ball Gloves

Tee Balls

and Tee Ball Bats

WE'RE ROUNDIN' THIRD AND HEADIN' FOR HOME!

Coming soon
to a store near you!
Official T●BALL USA
Athletic Footwear.

**Plymouth, a division of the
Chrysler Corporation, is the maker of
the Neon, Breeze and Voyager,
the official vehicles of T●BALL USA™.
Individual teams are supported
via local dealer sponsorships.**

References

Youth Sports Experts

Darrell J. Burnett, Ph.D.
Funagain Press
P.O. Box 7223
Laguna Niguel, CA 92607-7223
800/493-5943

Richard Blalock
Diamond Sports Park
4000 SW 122 Street
Gainesville, FL 32608
352/331-2345

Dr. Deborah Bright
Bright Enterprises, Inc.
915 Broadway
New York, NY 10010
212/533-5733

Major Robert A. Doss Jr. USMC
9911 Huntsman Path
Pensacola, FL 32514

Letha Y. Griffin, M.D.
Peachtree Orthopaedic Clinic
2001 Peachtree Road, NE
Atlanta, GA 30309
404/355-0743

Dr. Elliot Johnson
Winning Run Foundation
255B Settler's Road
Longview, TX 75605
903/663-6256

Dr. Lou Makarowski, Ph.D.
5120 Bayou Blvd., #6.
Pensacola, FL 32503
904/477-7181

The Organizations

National Alliance for Youth Sports
2050 Vista Parkway
West Palm Beach, FL 33411
407/684-1141

National Recreation and Parks
    Association
2775 S. Quincy Street, Suite 300
Arlington, VA 22206
703/820-4940

USA Baseball
2161 Greenwood Avenue
Trenton, NJ 08609
609/586-2381

YMCA of the USA
37 West Broad Street, Suite 600
Columbus, OH 43215
614/621-1231

IBA/International Baseball
    Association
Avenue de Mon Repos 24
Case Postale 131
1000 Lausanne 5, Switzerland
011-41-21-311-1863

Youth Baseball Leagues

Babe Ruth League, Inc.
1770 Brunswick Pike
Trenton, NJ 08638
609/695-1434

Dizzy Dean Baseball, Inc.
1213 Helena Drive
Hixson, TN 37343
615/875-0066

Dixie Youth Baseball, Inc.
P.O. Box 877
Marshall, TX 75671
800/256-8444

Little League Baseball, Inc.
P.O. Box 3485
Williamsport, PA 17701
717/326-1921

Little League Canada
235 Dale Avenue
Ottawa, Ontario K1G 0H6
613/731-3301

PONY Baseball, Inc.
P.O. Box 225
Washington, PA 15301-0225
412/225-1060

Tee Ball Baseball League
P.O. Box 643
Milton, FL 32572
904/623-4671

Youth Baseball Athletic League
3301 Alma Street
Palo Alto, CA 94306-3501
800/477-YBAL

Official Licensees

AA World Class
65 Ridgefield Avenue
Ridgefield, NJ 07657
210/313-0022

ADAMS USA
P.O. Box 489
Cookeville, TN 38503
615/526-2109

BIKE Athletic Company
2801 Red Dog Lane
P.O. Box 666
Knoxville, TX 37901
800/245-3231

DYOT
3245 Lamarque Drive
Cincinnati, OH 45236
513/891-9451

Houze Glass Corp.
P.O. Box 307
Point Marion, PA 15474
412/725-5231

J&A Enterprises
P.O. Box 3202
Amherst, MA 01004-3202
888/877-4440

Market Identity
P.O. Box 10540
Canoga Park, CA 91309
800/927-8070

Mercury International Trading
One Mercury Way
P.O. Box 222
North Attleboro, MA 02761-0222
508/699-9000

Outdoor Cap Company, Inc.
1200 Melissa Lane
Bentonville, AR 72712
800/797-0722

Spalding Sports Worldwide
425 Meadow Street
P.O. Box 901
Chicopee, MA 01021-0901
413/536-1200

World's Finest Chocolate, Inc.
4801 South Lawndale
Chicago, IL 60632-3062
312/847-4600

Publication

Baseball Parent
4437 Kingston Pike #2204
Knoxville, TN 37919-5226
423/523-1274

About the Author

H.W. "Bing" Broido is the author of the *Spalding Book of Rules*, a definitive guide to the basic regulations, officials' signals and playing fields of 40 popular sports. Following his consultations with the national governing bodies and federations responsible for each of the sports, Mr. Broido co-founded the T•BALL USA Association and is its president. A graduate of Dartmouth College, he heads a consumer products marketing firm developing merchandise programs in such areas as art, entertainment, fashion, fitness and collectibles. Married and the father of daughters, he is a popular speaker and lifelong sports enthusiast.

FREE

OFFICIAL T•BALL USA
MEMBERSHIP CARD

Become a member and be eligible for special benefits.

Membership card is personalized and has 10 T-Ball rules to remember on the back.

Player's name _____

League _____

Parent's name(s) _____

Address _____

City _____ State _____ Zip _____

CLIP AND MAIL TO: OR CALL:

T•BALL USA   **800/741-0845**
Suite 1901
915 Broadway
New York, NY 10010

Masters Press has a complete line of books to help coaches and participants alike "master their game." All of our books are available at better bookstores or by calling Masters Press at 1-800-9-SPORTS. Catalogs available by request.

Youth, Sports and Self Esteem

Dr. Darrell J. Burnett, Ph.D.

At last! A book for the parents of youth-leaguers that puts youth sports in proper perspective. Complete with colorful examples, cartoons, photographs and checklists. Endorsed by the National Youth Sports Coaches Association.

$12.95, ISBN 0-940279-80-0

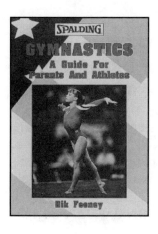

Gymnastics: A Guide for Parents & Athletes

Rik Feeney

Takes the beginning athlete and parent through the ups and downs of a gymnastics career. The most complete guide to the sport available. Approved by USA Gymnastics.

$14.95, ISBN 0-940279-43-6

Youth Strength and Conditioning

Matt Bryzcki

Takes the special needs of growing bodies into consideration, and shows parents, coaches, and kids how to safely improve nuscular strength. Part of the Spalding Youth League Series.

$12.95, ISBN1-57028-041-X

I Can Do Gymnastics:
Skills for Beginning
Gymnasts

USA Gymnastics
The safest and most effective way
to learn the basic gymnastic skills. A
must for every beginning gymnast.
$14.95, ISBN0-940279-51-7

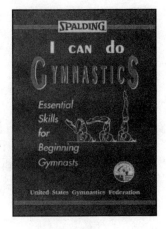

I Can Do Gymnastics:
Skills for Intermediate
Gymnasts

USA Gymnastics
The "next step" in gymnastics and
movement skills. Skills are combined
into movement sequences and alternative apparatus possibilities are ex-
plored.
$14.95, ISBN 0-940279-54-1

Youth League Baseball

Skip Bertman
Skip Bertman, coach of the 1991, 1993 and 1996 NCAA Cham-
pion LSU Tigers, devotes each chapter to a specific phase of the
game. Includes information on basic skills such as hitting and
catching, as well as on more complex matters such as position-
specific abilities. Part of the Spalding Youth League Series.
$12.95, ISBN 0-940279-68-1

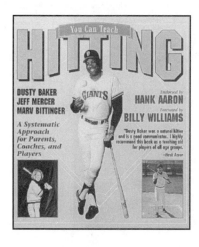

You Can Teach Hitting
Dusty Baker
with Jeff Mercer &
Marv Bittinger

Written by the acclaimed manager of the San Francisco Giants, this book is lavishly illustrated with four-color photographs and computer enhanced graphics throughout, and takes you from selecting your bat to selecting your pitch.

$24.95, ISBN 0-940279-73-8

Defensive Baseball
Rod Delmonico

Position-by-position as well as overall team strategies are presented in a concise, easy to understand format. Its photos and illustrations make this one of the best visual-aid instructional baseball books available.

$14.95, ISBN 1-57028-029-0

Heads-Up Baseball: Playing the Game
One Pitch at a Time
Ken Ravizza & Tom Hanson

"This book provides practical strategies for developing the mental skills which will help speed you to your full potential."

— Dave Winfield

(Introduction by Jim Abbott and foreword by Hank Aaron)

$14.95, ISBN 1-57028-021-5